Y0-BEA-487

French Piano Music

Da Capo Press Music Reprint Series

MUSIC EDITOR
BEA FRIEDLAND
Ph.D., City University of New York

FRENCH PIANO MUSIC

ALFRED CORTOT

Translated by
Hilda Andrews

DA CAPO PRESS • NEW YORK • 1977

Library of Congress Cataloging in Publication Data

Cortot, Alfred, 1877-1962.
    French piano music.

    (Da Capo Press music reprint series)
    Reprint of the 1932 ed. published by University
Press, Oxford.
    1. Piano music—History and criticism.
2. Music, French—History and criticism. I. Title.
ML724.C713 1977   786.4'04'10944   77-4108
ISBN 0-306-70896-5

This Da Capo Press edition of *French Piano Music*
is an unabridged republication of the first edition
published in London in 1932.

Published by Da Capo Press, Inc.
A Subsidiary of Plenum Publishing Corporation
227 West 17th Street, New York, N. Y. 10011

French Piano Music

ALFRED CORTOT

French Piano Music

Translated by

Hilda Andrews

First Series
Claude Debussy, César Franck
Gabriel Fauré, Emmanuel Chabrier
Paul Dukas

1932
OXFORD
UNIVERSITY PRESS
London : Humphrey Milford

OXFORD UNIVERSITY PRESS
AMEN HOUSE, E.C. 4
LONDON EDINBURGH GLASGOW
LEIPZIG NEW YORK TORONTO
MELBOURNE CAPETOWN BOMBAY
CALCUTTA MADRAS SHANGHAI
HYMPHREY MILFORD
PUBLISHER TO THE
UNIVERSITY

10 - 20 - 78

PRINTED IN GREAT BRITAIN AT THE UNIVERSITY PRESS, OXFORD
BY JOHN JOHNSON, PRINTER TO THE UNIVERSITY

PREFACE

THIS series of essays consists of a collection of studies originally written for the *Revue musicale* in the course of recent years. A second series will be devoted to the works of Saint-Saëns, Vincent d'Indy, Maurice Ravel, and others whose names cannot be excluded from a discussion of the leading pianistic influences of the French School.

I hope that the reader of the pages that follow will bear in mind the motive which prompted me to write them. These studies are, first and foremost, the notes of a pianist wishing to share his impressions, and to create in the listener a state of mental receptivity similar to his own. They aim not so much at a rigid musical analysis or discussion of the aesthetic question as at the expression of the poetical quality of the works concerned.

My purpose will be amply achieved if the reading of these commentaries stimulates some lovers of piano music to share my admiration for the wide variety of profound, lyrical, or picturesque compositions in which the creative genius of the musicians of our race has revealed itself, and which, as a whole, reflects one of the supreme moments in the musical history of France.

A. C.

CONTENTS

I

The Piano Music of Claude Debussy

THE technical novelty and inventiveness of Debussy's piano music has been often enough discussed. Critics have appraised the delicate audacities of this harmonic idiom as it reveals itself under the tests of the analyst, recognized the subtlety of a style of writing which discards conventional methods of modulation, allowing relationships of a sudden, exquisite intimacy between only distantly related keys, and have literally marvelled at the miracle of an art which is new both in matter and style simultaneously.

It is a fact that in the creation of a delicate harmonic tissue which suited his own sensibility and imagination, Debussy heightened the hearer's indefinable sensuous pleasure, and at the same time restored to piano technique a unique lyrical quality and a harmoniousness which, it seemed, French music had for the moment sacrificed in favour of the more austere idiom of the Franck school of composition.

This keen understanding of unusual instrumental resource, used with unerring felicity to create exactly the impression in the composer's mind, is as much to be seen in Debussy's orchestral works as in the quartet or in the three sonatas of the set that was unfortunately left incomplete. Sometimes we find it in the small detail of a particular accent, which in the service of an ingenious prevailing rhythm underlines some picturesque phrase with a touch both firm and delicate; sometimes in the use of unaccustomed registers which, by changing the timbre of instruments, adds depth of colour to many of the 'descriptive' pieces; or sometimes, again, it is in that fluid, transparent quality of his very personal harmonic backgrounds, whose tone fantasies seem gradually to unfold themselves, sensuous and intimate, before again dissolving.

All these effects or tone combinations, it is true, were common knowledge among virtuosi who had explored the boundaries of their art; but they had been used, as it were, as decorative devices outside the range of music proper. Only the amazing acuteness of perception of an artist as imaginatively sensuous as Debussy could discern the full use to be drawn from them, and embody these new elements with so unerring a taste, with such point and freedom, into a musical speech which was utterly his own. And in spite of the apparent impersonality of piano timbres, Debussy manages to evoke from the instrument tone-blends that exactly match his expressive needs, and in as individual a way as his use of the orchestra or of chamber music; and all this from his very first attempts.

In a remarkable article which appeared just after the first performance of *Pelléas*, Paul Dukas said that he found it impossible to analyse separately music so intimately allied to the poem, remarking that it would be like trying to gauge the effect of a stained glass window from the outside, without the necessary factor of light shining through.

Claude Debussy

Debussy's piano music, too, has its own persistent poetry which lives in it, softening or heightening its tones, quickening or relaxing its pace, imposing silence, inspiring detail, moulding proportions, and this hidden poetry is his imagination. Not only a musical imagination like Chopin's or Schumann's or Fauré's, sufficient to itself, and suggesting the dreams and desires of humanity without actually delineating them, but a precise imagination which uses the most clearly descriptive suggestion of emotion and spirit.

In the course of this essay I shall try to avoid splitting on Dukas's reef; but I must confess that it is a hazardous proceeding to attempt to combine with the description of so individual a musical idiom an analysis of the inner emotion which must dictate the expression of it.

But it may be that a provocative metaphor will give point and subtlety to the colour of a musical phrase, and that by stimulating the reader's imagination through suggested similes, I may prepare a more fertile soil, widen the range of his musical emotion; and though I cannot hope invariably to fathom the composer's exact meaning, the very fact of wishing to explain to myself the reasons for my liking may influence others in the same direction.

The first piano works were composed between 1888 and 1890: the two *Arabesques*, the *Ballade*, the *Mazurka*, the *Rêverie*, the *Nocturne*, and the *Valse romantique*. These only dimly suggest, it is true, that exquisite musical capacity, mistress of its powers, skilled creator of sensation, to be revealed in the *Préludes*, the *Estampes*, or the *Images*. For in spite of

the ingenious use of rhythms and timbres entirely
unfamiliar to the genre as seen in the work of most
of his contemporaries, Debussy here seems a little
sensitive, like all of them, to the combined influence
of Grieg and Massenet, who exercised a benevolent
tyranny over the whole epoch in the realm of so-
called drawing-room music. The charm of these
rather colourless compositions still smacks of the
school-room; and it is inconceivable that at the very
time when he was writing with so prudent a pen, the
Institut was feeling obliged to condemn the daring
propensities of the composer of *Printemps* and of
the *Damoiselle Élue*.

We have to wait several years more before being
given a real opportunity of appreciating that incisive,
translucent technique which makes Debussy's pianistic style not unlike the parallel art of Degas or of a
Chinese print; but at the same time among the productions of this period there are three separate
pieces which deserve special notice: the *Fantaisie* for
piano and orchestra, the *Suite Bergamasque*, and
Danse.

It is common knowledge that Debussy never
authorized the publication of the *Fantaisie* during his
lifetime; it was written in 1888, and formed the last
part of that 'envoi de Rome' of his which was so
unluckily received by the musical section of the
Institut; and afterwards he withdrew the work from
the programme of a concert of the Société Nationale
with the excuse that the orchestration of the finale
was incomplete.

There was ample chance, then, at the recent first

Claude Debussy

performance of this work, for several musicians to protest that it was sacrilege, though one would never have thought them so careful of Debussy's posthumous fame. But we can assure these estimable people that there is reason to suppose that the composer's reluctance to publish was not based on exclusively musical grounds.

In any case, even if we allow for a certain modesty on Debussy's part as far as various defects in orchestral technique are concerned—and not only in the finale; even if we deplore a faulty sense of proportion which curtails the last movement as well as the recapitulation and coda of the first, we can still maintain that the *Fantaisie* is much more than a merely promising work, as some criticisms have rather hastily assumed.

There is a freshness and freedom in the themes of the first movement, a dreamy, tender melancholy in the slow movement, a mysterious transition linking it to the finale, and a firmness of touch in this last part as it underlines the rhythmic changes of the initial theme, which stamps it as the work of a musician sure of himself, and conscious of his own musical personality, if not yet absolute master of an individual idiom.

It is illuminating to study the technique of the piano part—modelled on Vincent d'Indy's *Symphonie sur un thème montagnard*, where the piano is treated as a concerted rather than as a solo instrument—and to define the quality that distinguishes it from the later works of the same period, hinting at the sparkling technique of the descriptive pieces of the future; we find that it lies, unmistakably, in the manner of exploiting its particular timbre, and in the way in which the blending of the piano with the orchestra enriches and varies the statement of a musical phrase by the use of the piano's nimble virtuosity, effects of pedalling and the picturesque colour of its percussive tone.

The *Suite Bergamasque*, tinged softly with the hue of Verlaine, is less individual, and occasionally flavoured with Fauréisms, which do not, however, affect its real quality in the smallest degree; yet it comprises already the rather precious mélange of modern and antique which characterizes a number of Debussy's later pieces, and conjures up the delicate shades of the writers for the clavichord, his chosen ancestors.

He revives their ancient grace and manner here in their old purity, with a touch already of the felicitous idiom which was to present itself so elegantly in the suite called *Pour le Piano*, for instance, in *Mouvement* from the first series of *Images*, or again in the prelude called *Les Tierces Alternées*.

In the lightning caprice, the flashes of sun and shadow in the piece entitled *Danse*, originally called *Tarentelle Illyrienne*, we have an anticipatory glimpse of the bounding rhythm which was to infuse into Debussy's music so delicious a note of novel and personal joyousness. This is already the very pulse and tone of the *Collines d'Anacapri*, of *Masques*, of the *Cakewalk* from the *Children's Corner*; and the basic theme, almost note for note like the theme of the *Fantaisie* for piano and orchestra, heralds the lively twists and turns of the *Danse de Puck*.

Claude Debussy

If I were now to investigate the reason why these three works seem superior to Debussy's pianistic work of the same period, and so clearly suggest his mature style, I should point out that two of them, *Danse* and the *Suite Bergamasque*, are descriptive in type, creating sensations rather than sentiments, and that the value of the *Fantaisie* lies much more in the tone, colour, and play of rhythm than in the development of thematic ideas.

Here I have touched on one of the secrets of Debussy's incisive and penetrating genius.

He had so perfect a faculty for crystallizing in sound visual impressions, whether direct or suggested, by the imagination, by the plastic arts or by literature, that he could turn the full force of his art into a channel of sensations hitherto hardly ever opened to music at all.

It is rare to find him inspired by one of those emotions which since the revelation of Beethoven have stirred the soul of composers and inspired their works: that is, passion, grief, and human ardours. Not that he disdains or repudiates emotion in music; but a sort of patrician reticence leads him rather to suggest it by inference than to allow us directly to experience it.

And rather than work on our feelings by the poignancy of personal emotion, rather than create a tone-architecture of lovely line and form whose chaste restraint will suffice to satisfy us, he contrives, in a hidden sensuousness of linked chords, in the sinewy throb of a rhythm or the sudden mystery of a silence, to let fly this secret arrow whose delicious, subtle poison drugs us, almost without our realizing it, into the sensation which he deliberately intended; and we experience it as intensely as in actual reality.

An art whose mechanism was as refined as this and which implied such perfect mating of inspiration and method was naturally destined to be used in translating the rarest and subtlest of feelings. We shall accordingly observe that the performance of Debussy's work demands a more imaginative and sensitive co-operation, more delicately inflected, that any music had demanded before.

Others have talked of a Russian influence, and particularly of Moussorgsky's, in relation to this mode of expression, so alien to what our ears and our intellect are used to experience or to imagine, by which Debussy opens up to us the virgin loveliness of undreamt-of sensations. Indeed, in the orchestral works, certain methods of scoring, the frequent division of the strings, an individual use of wind and artificial forcing of its timbre, all bear witness to Debussy's frank relish for the inventive technique of Rimsky or Balakiref. But the question there at stake is only a passing resemblance in descriptive devices, and takes nothing whatever from the originality of writing nor from the inspiration. And we cannot accept the suggestion as a general inference when we compare the almost personal intimacy of Debussy's most significant piano works with the clearly external bias which all the compositions of the Russian school possess, with their lusty sensuality imported from the East, their romantic, 'folk'

Claude Debussy

feeling which exploits a deliberately unsophisticated musical exterior to mask a clever technique and a crafty sense of effect.

There remains Moussorgsky, for whose music Debussy indeed professed a wide sympathy, not unlike the feeling Robert Schumann once felt for the musical lyrics, so marvellously new, so full of emotion and unshed tears, of the Polish composer, Frederic Chopin. We shall find Debussy speaking of Moussorgsky's *Chambre d'enfant* with a very real sincerity, feeling the secret, sleeping force that lies within the tiny compass of these penetrating pages. And we know how often, by personal action quite unusual for him, he would stir his circle of friends to enthusiasm for *Boris Godunof* or for *Khovantchina*, which he was undoubtedly the first person in France to discover. But if now and then in Debussy's work there comes to light a resemblance of method or style to an art he admired so whole-heartedly, it only emphasizes the more the fundamental difference of race and mental culture which separates the two temperaments.

A gap of about ten years divides the works of his youth from the piano works in which Debussy's genius for descriptive suggestion was to be exercised in the future. Ten years filled with the plaintive tenderness which prompted *Pelléas*, with the warm ecstasy of the *Quartet*, with the sensual languor of the *Prélude à l'Après-midi d'un Faune*, the tonal novelties of the *Nocturnes*, where the reflection of sky and sea, and the subdued splendour of high-born merrymaking, seems by some miracle of orchestration to be born in the very music which describes it. Ten years in which Debussy worked his idiom, daily more plastic, by the patient practice of an art which the jaded eloquence of romanticism could never coarsen; while he stimulated his own imagination through contact with the literary style most akin to it, Baudelaire, Verlaine, and Stéphane Mallarmé, or through an emotion like Maeterlinck's which seems to float beneath the surface, and whose slumbering mystery his music brought to light.

To mark his return to piano music after this long pause, he wrote in 1901 the three pieces of a suite *Pour le Piano*; these reveal in a most captivating way the changes in his style since the works in his earlier manner, and can be considered a sort of transition between these early works and those later ones whose secret was already his to use.

The titles convey nothing: they are called *Prélude*, *Sarabande*, and *Toccata*, and in appearance suggest no more than the sparkle of clear tone, or—in the *Sarabande*—the serene nobility of grave antique harmonies. But the technique assumes a precise ingenuity, a variety of device, and a harmonic flavour so expressive that one seems to see fantasies already floating on the surface of a music hardly able to conceal them.[1]

[1] A correspondent, M. E. Rollin, has been good enough to point out that the *Sarabande* had appeared in 1896 in a Paris magazine called the *Grand Journal de Lundi*. It was announced as being part of a series of pieces to be published by Fromont and to bear the general title, already, of *Images*. This first version differs perceptibly from the final one, and bears the following indication of expression at the head of it: 'In a Sarabande movement—that is to say with slow serious

Claude Debussy

From 1903 till his death, piano compositions follow an almost uninterrupted sequence, and from this time on constitute the essence of his work, with the exception of a few songs, *Saint-Sébastien*, and two orchestral works, *La Mer* and the *Images*. And it must be remarked that these latter works only form the third series of a suite of pieces published under the same general title and the outcome of a single sentiment, though the first two sets were composed for the piano.

It was with the publication of the *Estampes* in 1903 that Debussy finally established the *genre* and the form of these profound or graceful works which gave the piano a new poetry, where bubbling laughter and murmured sighs, heard a thousand times in every vibrating note, whisper of an Ariel with invisible wings for whom the scented night holds no secrets, who hears every stirring of the wind on water, all the voices of the breeze, and every breath of human emotion.

From this phase on he prefers to evoke a mood by a title or an epigraph flexible enough not to harden the interpretation into a puerile effort of imitation, and yet clearly enough defined to describe the sort of expression necessary; and he only discarded this custom in his very last works, which seemed to hint at a third style: that of the *Sonates pour divers instruments*, and of the *Études pour piano*, in which the musical texture is the only interest.

The three pieces which form the set of *Estampes* elegance, rather like an old picture, or a memory of the Louvre, &c.'

present a happy example of this matching of the title to the character of the music, and show how the music mysteriously carries on the delicate stimulus to our imagination.

The first of these pieces, *Pagodes*, could have no other intention than to awaken in the mind's eye an impression of the architecture of the Far East by a rather conventional use of tone effects and exotic keys. But Debussy imposes no mere pictorial idea on our imagination; from the very first notes of the care-free, yet firm and forceful rhythm, which is used to decorate the slender design with its successions of fourths, thirds, and seconds, above motionless held notes in the syncopated accompaniment, his unique genius for suggestion awakens in the listener a trance-like, delicious longing for this clear, luminous country where gentle rites and traditional dances mingle with festivals of peach-trees, and the sophisticated, age-old customs of a remote civilization.

Soirée dans Grenade, again, holds far more than a simple description of nights in Spain and the usual enchantment of guitars and castanets; we feel here the sensuous throb of Southern passion in the restless scented air of the Alhambra gardens, an evening heavy with fragrance; hypnotic love-songs float through the amorous night from the Moorish quarter, singing of a passionate fate; and muffled Iberian rhythms beat to the dances of Spanish girls, beautiful, grave and proud.

The scent of sun-warmed thickets in the Paris parks, the sun shining through a light shower, comes

Claude Debussy

to us out of the *Jardins sous la pluie*. An 'Estampe', a mere impression, it is true, but so fine and penetrating that in spite of the continuous animation of the fingers on the keys, we detect the hint of a regret for a vanished happiness through the sad little plaint of a child's dance-song.

Masques and *L'Isle joyeuse* were written and published in 1904; they seem to indicate a momentary recapturing of the *genre* and form of the youthful pieces. *Masques* in particular contains various passages strikingly analogous to the piece called *Danse*, or to countless devices in the accompaniments of the early settings of Verlaine. They are both rather long in comparison with the usual small dimensions of Debussy's piano works. And in spite of their perfect polish and the pains taken to construct a normal musical development, or perhaps because of such pains, they seem to miss much of the engaging individuality of the works of the same period.

Yet in *Masques* we feel all the restless, gaudy riot of Italian comedy, Scaramouche with his pompous gestures, Cassandra and Zerbinetta, absurd and seductive, Pierrot dreaming in the moonlight, and Arlequin at Columbine's feet in the sheltering night. And the *Isle joyeuse* sets the snare of its laughter and easy delights for careless lovers, whose light barques lie up by its happy banks under the smiling regard of Watteau, Verlaine, and Chabrier, whom the sensual curves of this music inevitably bring to mind.

Again, what might be designated as the orchestral pianism of these pieces—for we lack a phrase to define more exactly the diverse combination of timbres which enliven them with a fantastic brilliance—is literally enchanting; Debussy has never surpassed the ease and certainty of touch which governs the play of rhythm here.

These two pieces are perfect in verve and ingenuity, musical grace and construction; yet in spite of all this, the rare delight which Debussy has taught us to expect eludes us a little; it may be that the subjects he selected erred in being too directly suggestive.

For indeed it is not without justice that Debussy has been considered as above all the musician of those mysterious subtleties of sensation where, as Verlaine put it, 'the undefinable and the definable touch'. He himself said that the quality which moved him most in certain musical works was the translation into musical feeling of what is invisible in nature.

And when instead of awakening in us, by the magical artifice and power of harmony and rhythm, one of those states of mental receptivity which opens our ears to the singer and our hearts to the hidden throbbing under the realities of things and people, Debussy paints a picture whose composition is arresting and obvious enough not to exact this intimate collaboration of our sensibility, we cannot help feeling in a sense that we are being deceived.

But after all is not this very fact—this sense that we have been cheated of something—the most convincing testimony of the depths fathomed in us by those slender accents of sublime poetry which are the individual essence of his music, bearing within them the inexpressible force of genius?

The two books of *Images* were published in 1905 and 1907 respectively, and are each composed of three pieces contrasting in type; they follow a tempo and key plan already observed in the *Suite* for piano and the *Estampes*. They are very significant of the deliberate and, from this point, final trend which urged Debussy towards a musical idiom as subtle as the sensations he wished to express, which henceforward were the only motive force of his form.

Pianistic virtuosity stood as it were for the element of atmosphere in which the play of tone was enveloped, overwhelmed, reduced, or crystallized. So novel a conception of the character and function of the instrument gives Debussy's piano technique an individual poetry which keeps it clearly distinguished, even superficially, from the inventive virtuosity of Liszt or Chopin, who are nevertheless its lineal ancestors.

With these two composers virtuoso decoration is used as accessory to the underlying melodic line, it is amplified from a theme, underlines a development, and generally increases the expressive dynamic life of the work; but Debussy's fluid idiom tends to subdue the outline, veil the harmonies, and almost lengthen out the silence.

At least three of the six pieces which make up the *Images* enable one to appreciate the peculiar flavour of this idiom and the aptness of its use. These are *Reflets dans l'eau* from the first set, and *Cloches à travers les feuilles* and *Poissons d'Or* from the second.

French Piano Music

Here in *Reflets dans l'eau* is the drowsy, floating, reflection of inverted images, stretching slowly out on the flickering mirror of musical tone, through luminous chords and skimming arpeggios. *Cloches à travers les feuilles* paints a tone picture of hardly stirring boughs lulled in a sweet silence, a tranquil green shade touched but not disturbed by far-off vibrations sustained, quivering, by the pedals. And in *Poissons d'Or* a sparkling vivacity flashes in moving water, a fleeting luminosity vanishes in passing reflections, a trembling, leaping life is unfolded before our eyes and ensnared by the magic of the music.[1]

The second *Image* of the second series, *Et la lune descend sur le temple qui fut*, can be added to these three pieces; it shares the same inspiration, although it lacks their technical versatility, and its suggested character is only interpreted through harmonic language and the use of pedals. In spite of the elaborate title the feeling of the piece is simple and profound; it matches the contemplative beauty of a place on which Time has set his hand, as the misty night falls on the dreamy silence of its ruins.

The *Hommage à Rameau* and *Mouvement*, which complete the first series of *Images*, are the expression of a feeling less definitely suggestive, and yet one cannot afford to pass over the slight stimulus to the imagination provided by their titles. It would

[1] *Poissons d'Or* was perhaps inspired by the Oriental embroidery that Debussy was so fond of, where the wild leaps of a water faun are represented in a rich fantastic handiwork of silk and gold.

Claude Debussy

perhaps be no error of sentimental exaggeration to imagine this gravely magnificent effusion of *Hommage à Rameau* extending its homage far beyond the limits of one chosen name, and symbolizing all the bright geniuses born of the soil of France, whose ancestry was so justly claimed by Claude Debussy, self-styled 'musicien français'. For this noble lyric springs from the depths of the soul of the race, inspired by a universal emotion to assume this dimension and this grave dignity. And the expressive amplification it seems to demand from the interpreter can surely only enhance the music which is able to inspire it.

The apparently casual design of repeated quavers enlivened and supported by a similar beat of triplets, makes the piece called *Mouvement* really the generative force of that idiom of rhythmic dominance of which Stravinsky, and after him Bartók, Casella, and several other young musicians, have made a self-consciously expedient use.

We shall not find it again in Debussy's work, it is true—this stubborn beat of a rhythm which persists to exasperation point with its incessant monotony, and crystallizes that implication of elemental, primeval force which is one of music's most recent, if not most characteristic acquisitions. The prevailing feeling of *Mouvement* is a sprightly gaiety, a temperate vigour, but nevertheless this quality just described is already clearly to be seen there.

The *Children's Corner*, published in 1908, brought a new inspiration of infinite charm and tenderness into Debussy's piano work; it is dedicated 'to my dear little Chouchou, with her father's apologies for what follows'.

And 'what follows' is so charmingly felt, full of daydreaming and roguishness and all the poetry of childhood, that it surpasses anything ever written under the inspiration of similar subjects—except the *Kinderscenen* of Schumann, Moussorgsky's *Chambre d'enfant*, or Gabriel Fauré's *Dolly*, that lovely trio which plumb untold depths of childish feeling, where intuition mingles with memory, and the tender smile of the onlooker is sometimes wet with tears.

I can think of no way of better describing the delicate pathos of Debussy's *Children's Corner* than by applying to Debussy himself the words he used to describe the *Chambre d'enfant* : He wrote the following in an article in the *Revue blanche* in 1901, on the subject of Moussorgsky : 'No one has ever touched the softer side of our nature in tenderer or profounder accents . . . never has so delicate an inspiration been translated in such simple terms; it is made up of tiny effects one after the other linked by some secret bond and by the wide vision of genius.'

There are the very words to define the inspiration and style of the *Children's Corner*. And the very fact of the kinship between these lines and the slender masterpiece in which, several years later, Debussy was himself to whisper to us the loving secret of paternal love, is singularly strong evidence in favour of the axiom that 'to understand is to equal'. However, apart from the initial bond of emotion, there is no resemblance of form or idiom between the two works.

Claude Debussy

Moussorgsky's melodies conjure up the warm, folk atmosphere of Slav childhood overflowing with fresh, unsophisticated gaiety. They evoke the aimless daydreams, the noisy display, the sudden tenderness and overwhelming gaiety which is a sore trial to the patience of a superstitious old Niania, inexhaustible source of fabulous fairy tales.

But Debussy portrays in the *Children's Corner* the quiet decorous games of a sophisticated little town girl, already a small coquette with her prudent frolics and coaxing ways; and her quicksilver caprices seem sometimes to be held well in check by the presence of a traditional English Nannie.

Can it be that Debussy meant to underline this point with a touch of amused and tender mockery, when he gave English names, matching the general title, to the six numbers which, according to his own description, make up the 'programme' of the *Children's Corner*? Those who know how fond he was, both in speech and thought, of a certain turn of veiled irony, cannot doubt that he meant to. But these pages have a precious and almost universal artistic quality, an arresting tenderness of feeling, which swamps every hint of satire, except a detail here and there to give these little sketches the likeness of the dearly-loved model.

The first bars of *Doctor Gradus ad Parnassum* flash on the vision an adorable picture of the child at the piano, giving a humorous turn to her frankly unequal struggle with the tedious complications of that wretched Muzio Clementi. What abysmal boredom and discouragement we observe! What an irrepres-

sible desire to snatch at any distraction, a sudden ray
of sunshine, a fly on the wall, a rose shedding its
leaves, is betrayed in these abrupt halts, this sulky
snail's pace! And then at the end a cheerful return
to liberty and games again at last!

Then, in *Jumbo's Lullaby*, we hear little stories
crooned over the stolid felt elephant, too big for the
small arms that clasp it. She tells him these stories
without putting them into words, her own make-
believe, this six-year-old Scheherazade dreaming,
broad awake, a vivid baby day-dream, more intense
than reality and more entrancing than a fairy tale.
And at the end, is the child or the toy—or perhaps
both—dropping off to sleep?

We must put down to Debussy's elementary
knowledge of the English language the small mistake which made him call the next piece *Serenade of
the Doll*, when the index at the beginning of the
series calls it *Serenade for the Doll*. The French translation gives the exact sense by calling it *Sérénade à la
poupée* and not *de la poupée*. It is admittedly a trifle, but
not without interest to the interpreter; for, instead of
the slightly caricatured conception of a toy serenade,
he may put into it all the whims, and fantastic pre-
tence of childish play, stared at by the fixed smile of
the new doll, which lies there motionless in the
position last given it by the child's caprice.

Snow is dancing. A small face pressed against the
window-pane of a cosy room, watching with a melancholy interest the snowflakes idly passing. What, she
wonders, becomes of the birds and flowers when it
snows? And when will the sun come out again?

Claude Debussy

The little Shepherd. Charming toy shepherd with a
funny little flock of sheep, just taken out of the box,
and smelling of nice new varnish, what secret poetry
you carry with you of that unknown shepherd life
your crude figure evokes, with its sylvan quiet, its
silence, and its distant horizons!

Golliwog's Cakewalk. Irregularly and gawkily, the
comic creature jerks along in a rhythm which deliberately shatters accents to pieces; such peals of
laughter and delicious gaiety punctuate its ludicrous
gait that one feels the hand that penned it quivering
with an inexpressible tenderness.

I need hardly point out the skill with which the
pianistic technique of the *Children's Corner* matches
its subject. There is practically no facile brilliance,
but an exquisite detail of colour and nuances, a kind
of frail perfection of idiom which equals the fragility
of the idea.

The year 1909 and the beginning of 1910 were
occupied with the scoring of the third series of
Images and the composition of several songs; there
are only two short pieces during this period to swell
Debussy's pianistic output—they do not add to its
glory—and to mark the gap between publication of
the *Children's Corner* and the *Préludes*.

The first of these pieces, called *Sur le nom d'Haydn*,
was destined for a musical supplement to the Revue
S.I.M. in 1910, which contained six sketches contributed by Debussy, Dukas, R. Hahn, V. d'Indy,
Ravel, and Widor, under the general title of *Hommage
à Haydn*. It was a sort of musical punning conceived
in the true German tradition, and the theme of these

pieces was formed by the notes of the letters of Haydn's name. Debussy's effort is pleasing and clever, without being, and moreover without trying to be, anything else.

In 1910 a valse was published entitled *La plus que lente*, half parody, half serious, and unquestionably without any significance. But in this same year which saw the blossoming of this poor flower, Debussy's genius proved itself more sensitively original, more sensitive, and more versatile than ever before, with the publication of the first book of the *Préludes*.

The romantic conception of the Prelude—the conception that flourished in the feverish imagination of Chopin—as the fiery, concentrated expression of a human emotion constrained only by the limit of its agony or of its passion, was to mean nothing to Debussy until altered to conform to the demands of a more objective art and a less impulsive spirit.

It is not that he was deaf to the arresting note of a music in which an anguished sorrow was liberated, or that he disdained the tumultuous force of a paroxysmic climax of sound; *Des pas sur la neige* or *Ce qu'a vu le vent de l'Ouest* is a convincing enough proof of that. But he never relaxed for it the perfect command over his emotions; and when he means to excite ours, it is not by the power of feverish passionate inspiration. On the contrary, in his last works he forces himself into this seeming reticence of feeling; and it creates not only the individual note in his piano music but also the peculiar pleasure we get from it. It makes infinitely persuasive demands on our understanding, and by sage choice of subjects induces it to an effort which is practically collaboration; it is content with a delicate impulsion, knowing that our imagination will multiply its feeling a hundredfold.

The Prelude was to provide Debussy with the resources of a form specially malleable to his inspiration when transmuted into this new expressive ideal; for it bore an improvisatory character, its very brevity held a poetic value, it made easy the expression of all sorts of musical themes without imposing on them the discipline of conventional development. And it is a fact that none of his piano works have mirrored more faithfully than the preludes the freshness and variety of an art whose suggestive power seems to remain as exquisite as ever.

There have been various attempts to write explanatory notes on the *Préludes*, especially in France and Italy. But I feel that I ought not to be deterred from a new analysis of Debussy's most important pianistic work by the fear of an inevitable coincidence of feeling or of phrase with these excellent essays; and apologizing for reiterations which the reader may discover, I hope that, in default of other merits, they may at least help to establish the suggestive precision of the musical composition which makes such coincidence likely.

The following notes deal with the twelve *Préludes* in the first book:

Danseuses de Delphes. They turn and pass, grave and silent, to the slow rhythm of harps, timbrels, and flutes. And in the mysterious shadow of the temple, heavy with the fragrant rising spirals of holy incense, is the invisible presence of a god wrapped in a tranquil dream of destiny.

Voiles. Boats lie to anchor in the shining port. Their sails flutter idly, and on the breeze which stirs them sweeps the flight of a white wing over the crooning sea towards the horizon bright with the setting sun.

Le Vent dans la plaine. The breeze flashes over the short grass, stirs the bushes, and the hedges cower before it; now and then in the young glory of the morning the growing corn bows in a long undulating wave before the onslaught of a fiercer gust.

Les sons et les parfums tournent dans l'air du soir. Here is the languid distress of the dying day, when perfumes wander in the air's caress and the confused vibrations in the atmosphere are gathered up by the advancing night; and—to keep to the meaning of Baudelaire's epigraph—all the sensuous intoxication of a swooning heart—to what end?

Les collines d'Anacapri. Movement in the bright morning, and a glimpse of the hills round Naples bathed in sunshine; the vivid rhythm of a tarantella unfolding to a careless popular refrain, the delicious age-old longing of an amorous melody vibrating in the brazen sky, jarring against the persistent and piercing note of a flute.

Des pas sur la neige. Over the melancholy frozen ground of a winter landscape which Debussy summons up in sound before us, footprints linger still when the absent friend has gone, and each one awakens the sad memory of a joy no more.

Claude Debussy

Ce qu'a vu le vent de l'Ouest. Through the luminous pallor of the dawn, or in the night's terror, is hurled the fearful vision of a hurricane; and over the angry sea cries of agony are thrown back by the waves.

La Fille aux cheveux de lin. This is a tender paraphrase of the Scottish song of Leconte de Lisle, singing the charm and sweetness of his distant love, 'sitting all among the flowering lucern-grass . . .'[1]

La Sérénade interrompue. A mocking nocturnal fantasy in the manner of Goya, expressing the diffident passion of a 'Novio', his love-songs under a closed window, his timid, peevish agitation at an unexpected sound, or at the passing of a band of noisy students, in a street near by; heard above a swaying, sinewy thrumming of guitars, in a rhythm that throbs already through the pages of *Iberia*.

La Cathédrale engloutie. An old Breton tale goes that once in a while in the clear morning light, when the sea is transparent, the cathedral of Ys, sleeping its enchanted sleep under the waves, rises from the depths of the ocean and of antique time. The bells chime slowly, we hear the priests solemnly intoning, and the illusion sinks again below the rocking sea.

---

[1] A recent sale of autographs enabled me to see the manuscript of an unpublished song bearing the same title. The manuscript is not dated, but the dedication to Mme Vasnier makes it possible to place it among Debussy's earliest works. The musical text has no resemblance to the Prelude here, and does not seem to me of any very rare quality.

And yet Debussy had been inclined to attach a real importance to this youthful work, as this dedicatory phrase shows: 'All my best capacity is to be found in this: look and see for yourself.'

Le Danse de Puck. In whimsical swiftness and airy mockery, this quicksilver spirit from Shakespeare flits about in play, vanishing and reappearing, amusing himself by teasing some country bumpkin, or tormenting a pair of lovers, then in a flash is gone.

Minstrels. This is a witty and jocular picture of the atmosphere of the music-hall. English clowns appear and tumble on the stage in clumsy attitudes, and gusts of sensuous music suggest the idle pleasure of an evening's amusement.

The twelve *Préludes* of the second book were published in 1913; they are inspired by similar pictorial impressions, though perhaps a little more mannered. The composition of several of them seems to have been initially stimulated by the fortuitous charm of a musical phrase to which a subject was fitted afterwards, rather than by the actual sensation that the music was to suggest. Here Debussy seems, therefore, to anticipate the writing of the later *Etudes* where he discards external ideas and impressions altogether for a harmonious graceful virtuosity and an essentially 'absolute' musical pleasure.

But although this new collection of *Préludes* shows clear traces of a move towards a fresh style, it is closely bound to the foregoing one by the prevailing unity of technique and delicacy of decoration; and we find there the same things to admire and to value, for the same reasons.

Brouillards. A mist of tone hanging in confused tonalities, superimposed on the minor second, gives a supernatural, phantom-like quality to the melodic line which tries to disentangle itself from it. Luminous moments now and then gleam like lighthouse flashes at once swallowed up in the fog, vanishing to leave us wandering more and more uncertainly in the mist.

Feuilles mortes. Dead leaves flutter and softly gyrate, dropping silently on to the ground; the sad splendour of the dying year seems to bear within it all the emotion of a long and wistful farewell.

La Puerta del Vino. Here is a brilliantly coloured picture of a noisy quarter in a Spanish town; a low tavern where mule-drivers loiter, shouting strident songs and beating with their hands to goad on the sinewy writhings of a black-haired dancing-girl.[1]

Les fées sont d'exquises danseuses. Expressed in the exquisite flash of gossamer virtuosity, ethereal forms flit by in the darting play of shadows, flames dance, and smoke rises in billowing wreaths, melting into the encircling air and sunlight.

Bruyère. The intimate woodland romance of undergrowth where the deep scent of the earth mingles with the flecks of sunlight through the leaves.

General Lavine eccentric. Here is all the incisive irony

[1] Actually we owe the inception of this astonishing piece to a postcard which Manuel de Falla sent to Debussy of the famous gate at Grenada known by this name. Debussy was so struck by the contrast of light and shade that he decided on the spot to describe it in music, with the remark: 'I shall make something of that.'

The suggestion of Spanish feeling in this prelude is made more remarkable by the fact that at this time Debussy had never crossed the Pyrenees. And at the most he only knew Fontarabia and St. Sebastian in the latter years of his life.

and verve of a Toulouse-Lautrec. It is the same old puppet that one has seen so often at the Folies-Bergère, with his coat several sizes too large and his mouth like a gaping scar, cleft by the set beatific smile. And above all the ungainly skip of his walk, punctuated by all the carefully stage-managed mishaps, and suddenly ended, like a released spring, by an amazing pirouette.

La Terrasse des Audiences du clair de lune. Under this slightly cryptic title,[1] whose ceremonious charm is rather like the flowery grace of certain Chinese legends, we have one of the most deeply musical and exquisitely expressive works that Debussy ever wrote. The first two or three notes of the popular tune *Au clair de la lune* are etherealized by a delicate harmony of sevenths, on which in a slow chromatic progression shafts of moonlight seem to fall, steeped in all the passionate unrest of the scented night and its sensuous delights.

Ondine. Those whose eyes are opened can see her rising half out of the streaming water in shy nudity, caressed by the shining waves. And those who can understand know how tender and alluring she is with her murmuring voice telling of the treasures and sea palaces beneath the waves and the sweetness of her love.

---

[1] Robert Godet, in the *Revue Musicale* of 1 May 1926, is convinced that this title was suggested by the perusal of a letter from India which appeared in the *Temps*, signed René Puaux; in it this association of words appeared that caught Debussy's fancy so strongly. But the expression also occurs twice in Pierre Loti's book *L'Inde sans les Anglais* (pp. 324 and 326).

Claude Debussy

Hommage à S. Pickwick, Esq. P.P.M.D.C. It is quite impossible to conceive of a wittier musical expression than this, not only of Dickens's hero, but also of Dickens's own style. It is his own ironic good humour, his genial wit; every bar of this piece finds its mark, from the comic use of *God Save the King* to the snatches of whistling in the last page, passing through all the variations of absent-minded seriousness, diffidence and complacency, that make up the humorous figure which is Samuel Pickwick, Esq.

Canope. The quiet, thoughtful lines of this piece have the same nobility and restraint as the antique funerary urn they serve to symbolize. And this sad, tender ditty, sung as if by a wailing flute, tells the deathless love of the boyish spirit whose secret passion sleeps here in these grey ashes, in a slumber that never forgets.

Les Tierces alternées. The technical manner, a legacy from the clavecinists, which is the germ of this fantasy, has been used by Debussy with charming ingenuity. In his hands it is not only the excuse for the play of musical style, but evokes a silky feline grace which in its turn forms the style. He plays with this round interval of a third as a cat plays with a ball, making it bounce and dashing after it into a corner, and then bringing it into play again with a swift little pat of his paw, after a moment of seeming indifference.

Feux d'artifice. This last *Prélude* is a veritable *tour de force* of impressionistic virtuosity. Curling smoke from Bengal lights shows an occasional splutter of sparks, rockets crackle and rise in a great parabola of stars, Catherine-wheels spin and multi-coloured lights burst into brilliance, and the night is full of sparkling colour. All the enchantment of the scene is portrayed in the music, and with the painter's trick for giving his picture a touch of character, Debussy slips in a note or two of the *Marseillaise* in the last two or three bars, evoking the rowdy romance of the dusty evenings of the Fourteenth of July.

In passing I must point out a peculiarity of the setting up of the two books of the *Préludes*, a thing Debussy rarely did: and that is that none of the titles are given till the end of each piece; it is as if he wished the reader to enjoy guessing at the idea expressed in the music, and felt that the confirmation of his discernment at the end would create a sort of intimate ebullience of emotion. It is a vivid little Mallarméesque device, which proves that the symbolism is of the purest, and whose contrived element of surprise could only last for a second.

Another point is that the *Préludes* have no dedication. However, it was rare for Debussy to dedicate his work. We can see there a fresh sign of his rather distant reticence, but no mark of indifference or conceit; he did not go as far as some of his contemporaries, and dedicate his works to himself to show how high an opinion he held of his own capacity; but he only consented to dedicate them as a proof of particularly tender feelings, of admiration or friendship. The dedications of the *Sonates*, or of the *Children's Corner*, or of the *Hommage à Rameau*, for instance, with names of intimate friends like

Claude Debussy

J.-E. Blanche, the etcher Charpentier, Louis Laloy, Ricardo Viñes, who was the first performer of most of his piano works, and still more Chopin, whose name is at the head of the *Études*, all these witness the fineness and certainty of his choice.

There can be no question of adding to the list of the piano works proper the roguish and charming diversion called the *Boîte à Joujoux*, a children's ballet in five scenes from the text and designs of André Hellé, that Debussy wrote in 1913. This plastic music, that follows and outlines the childish pranks on the stage, cannot be dissociated from the pantomime of artificial emotions and unreal existence that springs into life with the troupe of baby puppets. But it is an infinite pleasure just to follow the musical inventiveness and witty caprice of the piano part for its own sake; without ever going beyond the bounds of a decorous accompaniment, it has its being in a world of beguiling orchestral colour, and relishes its own humour in every bar.

The outbreak of war found Debussy in the grip of an incurable disease which he tried to hide from his friends by a sort of proud reserve; that curious external trait of a nature whose artistic reactions all betrayed a bright sensitiveness. The horror of events happening around him, more even than his illness, conspired to cramp an art which could only flow through the subtle, unfettered joys of the spirit, as much from conscious choice as from natural bent.

Nevertheless, the fact of war directly inspired two pieces, one in December 1914, written originally for piano and orchestrated afterwards, called *Berceuse héroïque*, and dedicated 'In homage to His Majesty King Albert I of Belgium and his soldiers'; and the other for voice with piano accompaniment, the *Noël des enfants qui n'ont plus de maison*, written in 1915. The *Berceuse héroïque* is a poignant, serious work, worthy of the sentiment that inspired it; the accent almost of Moussorgsky speaks in its tragic simplicity, as the voice of this homely *Brabançonne* attains sublime powers and re-echoes as the mighty clarion of a struggling people.

Unexpected work was to fill part of the last months of Debussy's life, half musical and half patriotic; and but for the war it would probably not have occupied his attention, but again it proved his predilection for things connected with the piano. He was asked by Jacques Durand, the publisher, to collaborate in a revision of the classics for a French edition to replace the foreign ones; he chose the re-edition of Chopin, for whom since his piano student days at the Conservatoire he had professed an admiration that never lessened, even during a phase when fashionable expediency urged 'advanced' musicians to pass over tendencies that certainly did not lie in the massive shadow of Wagnerism.

It is no use expecting analytical notes in this edition, nor suggestions for interpretation, fingering modifications, nor any indication that smacks of the academic. Debussy had a dislike almost amounting to contempt for this variety of parasitic commentary, and the preface to the *Études* is a pointed instance of it.

Claude Debussy

But he had a strong feeling for Chopin's delicate warmth of harmony and the purity of his melodic design, and if his corrections are not inspired by an exact understanding of his work, and affinity with it, they reveal a love that was sensitive to his genius. Moreover, in Debussy's circle of friends they used to be fond of saying that he played the piano like Chopin. And it is a fact that his touch was exquisitely fluent, sweet, and warm, made for delicate nuances and intimate expression, without a jarring or strident note. He used the pedal and particularly the blending of both pedals with infinite skill, and like Chopin he loved instruments of an almost slack ease of action. But this is a purely exterior resemblance, and the essence of either Chopin's or Debussy's profound musical personality was certainly by no means a mere matter of piano tone.

The twelve *Études pour piano* were written at the same time as this revision, during the summer of 1915; they are dedicated 'à la mémoire de Frédéric Chopin', a fact which shows how much interest Debussy had derived from this intimate association of several weeks' length with the ideas and the works of the Polish musician.

These are real exercises in technique, and each one deals exclusively with some particular difficulty; the first book with the 'five finger' exercise, exercises in thirds, fourths, sixths, octaves, eight finger exercises; and the second book deals with chromatic intervals, grace notes, reiterated notes, contrasted tone, extended arpeggios, and chords.

French Piano Music

Like Liszt and Chopin in works of a similar nature, Debussy seems thus to marshal in order the whole battery of technical difficulties which must be overcome in order to interpret his music in its proper pianistic way.

But he wrings from each of these dry academic studies such a variety of effects, and uses so ingeniously the musical character of these successions of intervals or deliberately symmetrical figures, working them out with fine originality of style and delicate sense for the natural poetry of the piano, that one after another they give the impression of being the easy result of an inspiration which could find no more natural idiom for expression; they are very far from seeming exercises in the solution of a given technical problem.

In tone combinations which the earlier works have made familiar and which so characteristically reveal Debussy's personality, there are here to be met a whole range of unexpected pianistic effects, seeming still more striking and original because there is no suggestion of any literary idea to explain their daring novelty.

And apart from its musical quality, this was the first work of its kind to formulate, under the aegis of a great name, the principles of modern piano technique; the technical merit of this work alone will suffice to create for Debussy a place whose inestimable academic importance to the piano professors of to-morrow would have astonished his ironic humour.

Such is Debussy's music for the piano. I must add

several pieces for four hands to the list, like the racy *Marche écossaise des Comtes de Ross,* written in 1891, and scored in 1908; the popular and charming *Petite Suite,* published in 1894, of which there is also an orchestral version, though not from Debussy's pen; and the *Six Épigraphes antiques* which appeared in 1915, slightly akin to some of the *Préludes.* Three pieces for two pianos collected under the title of *En Blanc et Noir* and composed in the middle of 1915, and a work of negligible importance, *D'un cahier d'esquisses,* for two hands, which appeared in 1903 in Brussels, close this list of works, all conceived in devotion for the instrument which, since the advent of Wagnerism, had been abandoned by most French composers in favour of more full-blooded and elaborate tonal resources.

During an inflated period when it seemed that music could only be expressed through the hundred voices of the orchestra, and according to the dramatic or philosophic demands of an imposing rite, we find a Claude Debussy or a Gabriel Fauré expressing emotion and wandering fantasy through the intimate medium of the piano, and their gentle and persuasive influence only served to reveal the better their refined and effortless originality of spirit. Claude Debussy restored to the young musicians of our country a taste for this art which is at once living, sensitive, intellectual, and restrained, valuable for quality of tone rather than for mass of tone, and whether picturesque, impulsive, or tender, always ordered by that perfect sense of balance which recreates form in composition and brings back the true character of the instrument; and on this account the composer of the *Préludes* and the *Images* well merits the glory he preferred above all other, it seems—to be remembered in our faithful hearts as 'Claude Debussy, musicien français'.

II

The Piano Music of César Franck

IT has already been pointed out as a peculiarity of César Franck's piano music that it is divided into two periods set exactly at the extreme ends of his musical career. The earlier period, from 1832 to 1846, that is, from early childhood till the time of his engagement, consists of a series of glib effusions written well within the bounds of the consciously declamatory style of the epoch. And it was a transitional epoch, cautiously feeling its way, embroiled in the struggle between the decadent influence of the Italian style and the fever of budding romanticism, confusing eloquence with verbosity, seeing in Hummel the successor of Beethoven, in Félicien David the rival of Berlioz, and assimilating with equal interest, not to say with equal incompetence, the astonishing pianistic genius and caustic force of a Franz Liszt and the feeble commonplaces of a Thalberg or a Moscheles.

After this, an interval of nearly forty years, in which Franck's inspiration seemed to need the medium of the piano no longer, finding its true expression, almost its only expression, in the mystic voice of that incense-laden music that sprang from religious faith. And then between 1883 and 1887, when he was past sixty, as though he wished to make up for his long silence at one stroke, he produced the four great masterpieces which are the ultimate confession of his art and religion, united in an inseverable bond: the *Prélude, Choral et Fugue*; the *Prélude, Aria et Final*; *Les Djinns*; and the *Variations symphoniques.*

In this essay we can, without disrespect or injustice, quickly pass over the works of Franck's youth, written either in his school-days or at the time of his first successes as a pianist. They indicate practically nothing of his style and personality, and only their documentary interest would make them worth analysis. Here it will suffice to give their names, using the classification established by M. Vincent d'Indy in the work he reverently devoted to his master's memory; to this M. Julien Tiersot has just added a new and valuable contribution,[1] after the study of several manuscripts still in the possession of César Franck's family. There is therefore every reason to suppose that the list of piano works of the first period is now finally complete.

They are as follows: in 1832, *Variations brillantes sur l'air du Pré-aux-Clercs, Souvenirs du jeune âge,* composed for the piano by César Franck, aged eleven and a half, Op. 5; a quite well developed and successful piece stimulating its young composer with so lively a sense of satisfaction that he at once made a second version, for piano and orchestra.

In 1835: *Première Grande Sonate,* dedicated to Joseph Franck, and composed by his son César-Auguste Franck, of Liège, aged twelve, Op. 10; then

---

[1] *Les œuvres inédites de César Franck,* from the *Revue Musicale* of 1 Dec. 1923. It must be added that M. Servières had already, in 1897, attempted a classification of Franck's works, including, similarly, the unpublished compositions.

the *Première Grande Fantaisie*, Op. 12, in a single movement; two *Mélodies* for the piano, Op. 15; finally
a *Deuxième Sonate*, Op. 18, in which M. Tiersot already
traces the use of the cyclic form of which Franck
was to make remarkable use, with all its expressive
possibilities, in the Trio in F sharp minor written
several years later. All these childish compositions
have remained in manuscript and are included among
the works mentioned by M. Julien Tiersot.[1]

Then in 1842 an *Églogue* appeared, with the German sub-title of *Hirten-Gedicht*, whose pastoral calm
is only disturbed by a liberally descriptive storm, and
a Duo for four hands on the theme of *God Save the
King*, both published by Schlesinger; in 1843, a
Grand Caprice published by Lemoine, in my opinion
the most individual of this series of piano pieces, and
a *Souvenir d'Aix-la-Chapelle*, published by Schuberth
of Leipzig. Both the *Caprice* and the *Églogue* are
the outcome of a most convinced Lisztian feeling,
showing effects of alternating octaves, division of
the melody between the two hands, imitation of the
'voix céleste' stop on the organ; in short, they em-
ploy a regular machinery of virtuosity in the best
traditions of the moment.

In 1844, a very productive year, Franck transcribed four of Schubert's loveliest melodies for the

[1] M. d'Indy, in his revised study of Franck's works, has
published (Oliver Ditson & Co., New York, 1922) three short
piano pieces noted down at the end of a manuscript exercise-
book of counterpoint studies made under the direction of
Antoine Reicha, from 1835–6. These are harmless little
melodies labelled with youthful complacency: *Chants de moi,
réalisés*.

piano, on the model of Liszt: *Die junge Nonne, Die Forelle, Des Mädchens Klage, Das Zügenglöcklein,* printed by Challiot; he wrote a Ballade, which M. d'Indy supposed to have been published, but which we should never have known had he not been at pains to give us, in the Ditson edition, an accurate version of the original manuscript; and two *Fantaisies sur Gulistan,* Dalayrac's opera, published by Richault, in which once more Franck drops to the taste of the day. There is also a *Solo de piano avec accompagnement de quatuor* ascribed to this same year and numbered 10 in a list of his works that he himself compiled. M. d'Indy found no trace of this, in spite of careful research; but M. Tiersot, more fortunate, has been able to identify the composition, which was never published, as a *Fantaisie,* or more accurately, a *Méditation* on the themes of *Ruth,* the oratorio on which Franck was working at the same time.

In the catalogue in question this piece had already usurped the place of the *Première Sonate,* and is among those which their composer deprived of their temporary status, fifteen years or so later, by removing their original opus numbers from them in order to instate several other new pieces, among them the Mass for three voices and the six pieces for organ.

It was then that he discarded, in favour of maturer works, a *Fantaisie,* Op. 13, announced to appear in 1844, three childish pieces dated 1845, with the unassuming and almost derogatory title of *Trois petits riens,* which piece of modesty nevertheless did not save them from being finally thrown out—a *Fantaisie sur deux airs polonais,* published in 1845 by

Richault, and a Duo for four hands, published the following year, on themes from Grétry's attractive comic opera, *Lucile*.

'César-Auguste Franck of Liège', as he studiously signed all his first compositions—perhaps to distinguish himself from one Édouard Franck, a contemporary, also a pianist and composer, who lived in Berlin, but more likely from a characteristically methodical habit of mind—quietly closed the pianistic activity of his youth at a significant moment with two works written at the time of his becoming engaged, symbolically, as it were, standing at the threshold of a new life; these were two *Mélodies* in the form of 'Romances sans paroles', never published, and dedicated 'à Félicité'—the Christian name of Mlle Desmousseaux, whom he married in 1848.

We have to wait from this moment for little short of forty years, when he had become 'le Père Franck', as his pupils affectionately called him, before finding any new piano works from his pen. There is one insignificant trifle published in 1865 under the title of *Les plaintes d'une poupée*, a title which indicates both the age of the person for whom it was written, and the probable object in writing it; one or two arrangements of pieces originally written for the organ or for orchestra, a few accompaniments to songs, and the solo part of the fine piano quintet; and these constitute the rare exceptions to his apparent indifference or neglect.

It was an extraordinary break, as drastic as it was enduring; it is still more remarkable in that it fol-

lowed straight on after a phase of particularly prolific composition for the piano; for of the seventeen
opus numbers that represent Franck's work at the time
it happened, thirteen are written for the instrument
threatened with neglect, and the four others need
its co-operation; and this without including in the
list the unpublished pieces classified by M. Tiersot.

Aesthetic reasons alone, we have to admit, are
not enough to explain away so wholesale and so
sudden a schism. But after all, the search for the root
causes that involved pianistic bankruptcy for forty
years will not end without in some way illuminating
for us the works we propose to study.

As a matter of fact, the apparent artistic bias to
which I have just referred cannot be entirely dissociated from a deferential submission to paternal
wishes. All the evidence concurs on this point, that
the little bank clerk of Liège did not undertake the
musical education of his two children, César-Auguste
and Joseph, so much in response to their genuine
vocation as to be able to put their young talents to
the best possible profit, in the fullest and most
direct sense of the word. It was, moreover, as complete an education as his modest means allowed, including the special study of the piano for the elder,
and for Joseph, the younger, of the violin; with
advanced lessons in theory as well. And this careful
distribution of ability, in a time which was the golden
age of the 'duo concertant', gives us a further insight
into these far-sighted family plans. At the best it
reflects a sentiment very typical of the moment, if we are

César Franck

to believe the avowal of Henri Herz, then fashionable
pianist and composer, and at the same time publisher,
famous professor, and celebrated piano-maker,—in
short, thoroughly qualified to know. The following
fragment is quoted from a letter of his: 'There is no
family living whose vanity would not be tickled by
having one or two baby virtuosi for its own kith
and kin.'

If we add to the feeling of satisfied *amour-propre*
a few less disinterested motives, we shall have the
initial impulse behind not only César Franck's
musical career, but countless others of the same
period. The elder Franck probably looked on his
own sacrifices, to use the language of his profession,
as nothing more than the deposit necessary for the
success of a transaction in which he pledged his son's
future as well as his own savings.

But if his ambition did not aspire to fine artistic
ends, at least it was eminently practical. In 1833, as
soon as César-Auguste, the more gifted of the two
brothers, was ready to appear in public, we find him
embarking on a round of concerts organized by his
father; the child was then hardly eleven years old,
his father keenly alert, on the watch not only for
enthusiastic receptions but also for the more substantial results which in his eyes were the supreme issue.

In spite of the prodigious dexterity of the boy's
playing, and although he appeared before his
audiences interpreting his own works—a point
then held to be an essential part of musical talent—
yet the success of this first attempt fell a little short
of parental hopes. His father decided thereupon to

make a move to the place where all reputations were born, where every genius went to devote himself to finishing study; and as this sort of finishing study was necessary to the success of two virtuosi in the making, in 1835, the Franck family went to Paris.

The young pianist went through Zimmermann's course at the Conservatoire, and won in 1839 a big *prix d'honneur* in rather strange circumstances, which M. d'Indy has related to us. In 1840 he added to it a first prize for fugue, and in 1841 a second prize for organ.

In the following year, and, as always, in response to continual pressure from relations whose purpose was unchanging, he had to break off his pupil studies, leave his preparation for the *prix de Rome* examination, and take up the composition of *pièces d'occasion*; this, like his previous career as a pianist, was with the objective of winning fame and money from the public. The result was the collection of pieces with titles surprising from such a pen, these Fantaisies in the form of pot-pourris, these Souvenirs d'Aix-la-Chapelle, these Duos which need only the qualifying epithet of 'brilliant' to reveal not only their nature but the kind of success which, spurred on by parental instigation, they were to draw. Let us remember, to the credit of the younger Franck, that he does not seem to have exerted himself with any great conviction to earn the deplorable successes which his family hoped for; and the few really interesting piano pieces we meet among his earlier compositions are remarkable for a seriousness quite extraordinary for the period.

César Franck

In general, and in the choice of titles, he yields to the aesthetic fashion of the day; but already, in default of a more significant originality, he shows a fine disdain for currying popular favour.

Certainly there is nothing of the breadth of construction, the feeling for the wide sweep of phrase, the logical progress, which were the indelible hallmarks of the later works; there is *naïveté* and sometimes a certain clumsiness in his harmonic speech, steeped in academic method, that the expressive chromaticism of his riper talent has not yet enriched and extended; influences are to be felt that are to last for years—Weber, Grétry, Liszt, Meyerbeer, and these latter two above all when it is a question of a dramatic turn to a rhythm or the quickening of a melody. The form of his compositions changed so little that M. d'Indy has been able to define all the works of the first period under a single head: an allegro, framed between two expositions of the same theme, and the whole preceded by a short introduction. In summary, and remembering that in the various tendencies which are revealed in this embryonic state of musical thought we find genuine quality of the highest order, we cannot really be surprised that Franck, in his short career as a pianist and in the interpretation of his own works, never won the vulgar triumphs that were intended to make him the darling of the public—attaining the paternal goal—and the rival of the great. We can look in vain, in these works openly destined for the salon and platform, for the glib trappings of grace notes and tremoli, debased progressions, the flowery *cadenzas*, in a word for the elements of virtuoso performance without which in 1840 a pianist could never hope to enchant the crowd. I have already pointed out how in the *Grand Caprice*, published in 1843, Franck showed himself not altogether insensitive to the charms of the fashionable style; but even while the young composer exerted his best efforts to fall in with a project whose utilitarian side he was never allowed to forget for a moment, he seems nevertheless to be inhibited by some subconscious resistance from giving himself up to it so wholly as to be really successful. We have no grounds for reproach.

Also, he was not allowed to keep within the bound of his own compositions; I have in my hand the programme of a concert given at Liège in 1843 by the 'Frères Franck', which shows to what sort of jobs paternal ambition condemned the future composer of the *Béatitudes* and the *Symphony*. Here is a Duo for piano and violin on themes from the *Huguenots*, composed—if that is the right word!—by Thalberg and Bériot, for the two brothers to perform, jostling with a *Fantaisie sur deux airs russes* for piano arranged by Thalberg alone and performed by César-Auguste Franck; a *Fantaisie-Caprice* by Vieuxtemps, played by Joseph Franck. And to increase the artistic interest of the occasion, a work called a *Chœur des Buveurs* from the pen of one Birmann was to be sung by members of the Société d'Orphée, and also a *Finale* which even its performers tacitly confessed to be unworthy of posterity's attention, seeing that it bears no composer's name at all.

César Franck

As a curtain-raiser, with the aid of a local 'cellist, they played one of the Trios that César Franck had just finished, labelled *Trio de salon* for the occasion, no doubt in order not to scare away the audience.

We can reasonably accept this programme as an average example of this type of enterprise. That sort of thing was what the practice of his art meant to Franck the virtuoso. It was for occasions like this that he was forced to produce and perform music, for audiences which liked such motley shows, Philistines, as the irate Robert Schumann was then busy stigmatizing them from the other side of the Rhine. And all the time he was already planning out *Ruth*; he had just finished writing the surprising *Trio in F sharp*, and was sketching out a long orchestral piece on Victor Hugo's verses—*Ce qu'on entend sur la montagne*, a kind of symphonic tone poem, which remained unpublished, but which, if we are to judge by the extracts published by M. Tiersot, would be found to surpass anything that has been written in this *genre*, even the similar production of Liszt.

It would be a legitimate process of cause and effect, then, for Franck to conceive a detestation for the instrument which was indirectly and innocently responsible for such sordid manifestations of music. We are driven to consider his early acceptance of the drudgery of teaching which tied him all his life as a real effort towards liberation of spirit and intellect. It enabled him still to help the family finances, for he remained materially attached to the tutelage which filial scruples bound him to respect, but at the same time at least he would contrive to find time, perhaps between two lessons, when a pupil by happy chance was unexpectedly absent, to write a few bars more of whatever composition was in hand, without the worry of those *pièces d'occasion* which had burdened him from childhood.

Ruth, the candid oratorio for which he cherished a peculiar emotional regard all his life, was composed under these conditions, though not published until twenty-five years later. It was as though he was anxious to draw a definite dividing line between his previous production and what it was to become when, to use his own phrase, he could work at it; and he did it with a composition after his own heart.

A double event, in 1848, enabled him to establish his independence and maintain his artistic preferences. He married against his parents' wishes, and became organist at the church of Saint-François du Marais. Here was an end for him at last of the pianistic illustration of 'favourite themes' of varying descriptions and nationalities, the Variations on God Save the King or the Queen, following the vicissitudes of royal succession; never again need he be subjected to the public execution of a hotchpotch of scales, trills, and arpeggios, glorified by the name of music. He had found his *métier*: the modest duties that devolved on him were the pledge of a life according to his own liking, serious, temperate, and careful of the discipline of everyday routine. His future masterpieces are already there, awaiting their hour, in the patient shadow of his church.

* * *

César Franck

The evolution of the pianoforte at the end of the eighteenth century, and still more at the beginning of the nineteenth, was accompanied by a striking expansion of musical thought. New expressive or dramatic possibilities, unknown to the limited, exquisite poetry of the clavichord, were awakened by the tonal resources of the new instrument, its rich timbre, its variety, and most of all by its power of sustaining certain notes or harmonies over a long period.

Among the sentiments that the literature of the piano has tried from the beginning to express is the mystic sentiment of religion, confined hitherto almost exclusively to the atmosphere of holy places, organ music and concerts of sacred works. Through the piano that essence of the divine is fused into the familiar music, as it were, of daily life, ennobling it, stirring the Beethoven sonata to birth from the great philosophical reverie where the strivings of a restless soul were laid bare, filling the melody of Schubert with a sad and persuasive resignation, stimulating Liszt to fervour, lifting now and then the harmonious grace of Mendelssohn to the sublime, and uniting with emotional exaltation to infuse an ineffable tenderness into the music of Chopin and Schumann.

It was Franck's part to add to this inspired music the impulse to prayer, the *Prélude, Choral et Fugue,* and the *Prélude, Aria et Finale,* in so far as works of art are acts of faith.

Not that I subscribe for my part to the favourite legend of a mystic César Franck, a sort of Pater

French Piano Music

Seraphicus lost in dreams of heaven, illumined with
the ecstatic contemplative fervour which removed
him from the pricks and realities of life. The
nobility of Franck's life, reflected perfectly in the
beauty of his work, was precisely that he neither
shook off reality nor despised the affairs of humanity,
but rose above them. And, however urgent and
overwhelming they might sometimes be, he never
allowed them to dim the sacred flame of inspiration,
nor weaken within him his passionate love of music.

It would obviously be as unwarrantable as ridiculous, and, what is worse, incorrect, to underrate
the influence of Franck's religious belief on his artistic
production, and I am not attempting to do so. But
I should like to suggest that the particular emotion
revealed in his work, at least during the second half
of his life, has its mainspring in a clear aesthetic
belief as much as in the desire to make a profession
of faith; and that certain professional habits acquired in the course of a long career had, by an
almost inevitable repercussion, a definite influence
on his style of writing, even without his realizing it.

M. André Schaeffner has written an excellent
thesis on the various aspects of Franck's imprint
on contemporary music, very clearly pointing out
that the almost daily necessity for adjusting his improvisations, both in length and character, to the
different liturgical offices, had undoubtedly helped
to develop in Franck that sense of balance and logical
construction which already, and instinctively, his
earlier works had revealed. He demonstrates that
the ecclesiastical craftsmanship that links Franck

directly with his ancestors Bach and Buxtehude, and even the restrictions of his musical appointment had by no means stifled his imagination or dimmed his artistic inspiration, but, on the contrary, had enriched and strengthened it from resources most appropriate and natural to its character; he shows, in fact, that his whole musical work bears the stamp of a profession. The origins of the tonal and harmonic system in the big works of the last period can therefore be clearly derived from his regular and intimate acquaintance with the liturgical modes. I am quoting from memory and while, I believe, stating the essential drift of M. Schaeffner's argument, offer an apology for the absence of literal quotation.

As a matter of fact, the strong and individual flavour of Gregorian chant was able, more easily and perhaps more deeply than any other, to penetrate a musical language like Franck's, already prepared to assimilate it by the discipline of strict counterpoint, in which he had excelled as a student; to such a point, even, that he had offered his fiancée a four-part fugue as a startling testimony of his affection. The Conservatoire Library possesses this odd manuscript, in which the counter-subject provides the theme of a new combination of parts which is superimposed on the first.

With any one but Franck these hidden influences of plain-chant would have come to the surface only as the brand of a profession; but with him they are idealized, keeping only the essential rhythmic grandeur of the responses and the grave purity of their melody; and of the traditional harmonization which in his time wrapped it round (this was before the *motu proprio*, and Saint-Saëns and Charles Bordes had still to bring back the bare nobility of plain-chant) there remain only the elements akin to his own poetic gift.

Instinctively he disdained and rejected as unworthy of his art any picturesque or verbose trait which might alter a curve or destroy a proportion; a point mentioned before in the short sketch of his first piano works. As he grew older, to this purism was joined a desire for spiritual perfection, which urged him only to express sentiments refined to their noblest and most elevated form.

A remark made to an intimate friend of mine, who had the pleasure and the privilege of being taught by the great composer, touches very significantly on this: the subject under discussion was *Psyché*, and the delicately inflamed ecstasy disclosed in certain parts of the score; Franck placed his hand on a copy of the *Béatitudes* and remarked naïvely: 'What I like about this is that it does not contain a single sensuous line.' It would be difficult to express an artistic principle in fewer words or more precisely. For here it is the musician himself who speaks; and we understand what he means, and that this remark does not smack in the least of conventional morality. But if we add to the aesthetic taste that it reveals in the artist the sentiment that it betrays in the man—that quiet security of a faith which sets the idea of God as the perfect pattern and the ultimate end of all desire—we shall understand how naturally and unconsciously his music is the echo of his religious aspirations.

It has already been remarked—and the point confirms my own feeling—that it is by no means in his avowedly sacred compositions, the various masses, the motets, or the prose liturgies, that he fathoms the profoundest or most moving depths of Christian emotion. On the contrary, the works which belong to what we are accustomed to call absolute music are steeped in a sublime ecstasy in which one cannot help sharing—the Symphony, for instance, the Sonata for piano and violin that Eugène Ysaye received as a wedding ode on the day of his marriage, the Quartet, and the later piano pieces; or still more the works which, like the *Béatitudes* or the *Rédemption*, are based on texts one would hesitate to call literary, and whose sole merit lies in suggesting to Franck's imagination the opportunity to express the feelings of a humanity torn with emotion at the sufferings of its Saviour—with infinite tenderness and impassioned grief. On every page of these profound works Franck might have written *Soli Deo Gloriam*, that reverent assurance of faith with which the old masters used to sign their works, testifying to their humility of spirit and incorruptible belief.

But it is above all through a study of the organ works, shot through with contemplation and thought, that we come nearest to this blended ideal where the various elements that form Franck's style fuse and unite at the height of their significance in the crucible of inspiration. The piano works are their direct outcome, and it is these organ pieces, before any, that must be examined by the musician anxious to interpret the piano compositions in their authentic spirit.

It is these that mirror the reflections of inner being, meditative and passionately restrained within the bounds of spirit and faith, revealed again in the music I am going to attempt to analyse. Out of these works emanates the touching simplicity of the quiet, imploring chromaticism, condensed within itself, that we find later in the *Prélude, Choral et Fugue*, and in the *Prélude, Aria et Finale*; one might describe it as static, in contrast with the dynamic, fiery chromaticism of Liszt or Wagner.

The idiom of these organ pieces is entirely adapted to the resources of the instrument that had become, by choice as much as by necessity, Franck's daily companion, the glorious confidant of his art; it heralded the technique by which in due course he was to bestow a new nobility upon the timbre of the piano, adjust to the vibrating impact of the hammer the sustained stretches of the glorious music he poured forth from his organ-loft, music passionate with hope and certainty, music that raised suppliant or benedictory hands in prayer, music thundering forth prophecies.

We shall hear its echo in the inspired works that César Franck devoted, in the last blossoming of his career, to the long forsaken memory of his musical début.

If we try to establish the reasons for the late-flowering interest that turned Franck once more

César Franck

towards the piano, we shall find a natural consequence at once artistic and spiritual, analogous to the
one that forty years previously, working in inverse
order, had determined its neglect.

M. Vincent d'Indy, who was an authoritative witness
of this last period of the master's life, tells how in
the spring of 1884 Franck remarked to his pupils
that he wished he could endow with one or two
big works the literature of the piano, decadent and
sterile as it had become beneath the avalanche of
fantaisies and concertos which the first half of the
nineteenth century had showered upon it. This is
M. d'Indy's account, and for my part I see nothing
in this quite personal statement—any more than in
a subsequent commentary on romanticism and the
artistic merit of its gift to music—which leads us to
suppose that Franck expressed himself thus, or with
so marked a candour, on the subject of a period
when the piano, it is true, reigned supreme; he by
no means intended, I think, the general disparage-
ment of its music.

The first half of the nineteenth century, from the
point of view of pianism, includes the interval between the last sonatas of Beethoven to the first
works of Brahms, taking in the music of Weber,
Schubert, Mendelssohn, Chopin, Schumann, and
Liszt. Surely this represents a fine enough harvest
of masterpieces in vindication of the instrument, and
of the genre that inspired them, to justify a less
stringent criticism; and surely we cannot imagine
that Franck, who taught the technique of the piano
all his life to privileged pupils, and with an interest

that never waned, would not have confirmed it. I know that M. d'Indy is anxious to extol the nobility of inspiration and formal beauty that his master's works reveal, and sets them in his mind as the opposite extreme from those shocking effusions I have already deprecated for their empty affectation and their vicious influence on public taste. And I have similarly pointed out that Franck's withdrawal from a pianistic career, whether as composer or virtuoso, was to escape their degrading contamination. But I feel that M. d'Indy's reverent zeal errs by overstatement when he says that 'no composer had advanced beyond Beethoven, and while the technique and idiom for the piano had transcended all bounds, the music written for it had degenerated in quality'. He includes in a general confused censure—and, as it were, with Franck's tacit consent—all the great masters, of whom Franck was the lineal successor, with the licensed purveyors of stuff to glut the appetite of the crowd, drawing-room entertainers and boarding-school hacks; and the result is that he is wrongly led to the drastic conclusion I have just quoted.

Though his origins unfortunately condemn him irreparably in M. d'Indy's eyes, Mendelssohn, that fine, pure artist, played a more energetic and conspicuous part than Franck in the struggle against the music-mongers who were degrading the music of his age; the very title of the *Variations sérieuses*, or the motive which impelled him to compose the noble E minor Fugue at the bedside of a dying friend, can be taken as the index of an aesthetic and moral quality worthy of the master of Sainte-Clotilde. Schumann, again, by his music as much as by his writings, led a passionate revolt against the Philistines; and did not Liszt also, in a large measure, plan out the route that César Franck was to follow—the Liszt of the Sonata, the *Méditations poétiques et religieuses*, and the *Légendes*, and above all the noble Variations on 'Weinen, Klagen, Sorgen', which anticipate, as much by curious thematic analogy as by the general feeling of the work, the equally noble *Prélude, Choral et Fugue*?

I can follow M. d'Indy better when he keeps to a period nearer our own and assigns his master's renewed interest in the piano to a desire to see it profit by the great stirring of musical activity after the 1870 war, manifested in France by the creation of the Société Nationale de Musique. I am sure that in undertaking the composition of the four works under discussion Franck was not so much protesting against the so-called morbid tendencies of the beginning of the century (for it is hard to imagine Franck writing music in protest against anything), as bent on proving the expressive worth of an instrument unjustly neglected or disparaged at the actual moment of which I am writing. A whole generation of French composers had turned towards a symphonic or dramatic idiom, magnetized by the budding influence of Wagnerism, the expansion of programme music, and the infatuation for the picturesque and the romantic; perhaps even, after the clash of political issues, they were inspired by the secret— and salutary—ambition to rival the victors of yesterday on their own artistic ground; and this meant the neglect of a musical medium less showy, but none the less important for the country's musical health.

The example of a man like César Franck, then, whose moral influence was already felt outside the limits of the coterie, was bound to be interpreted, at least by his satellites, as a sort of profession of faith, and to plead by its very existence for a musical style curiously alien to prevailing ideas. And, since 1886, we notice his greatest pupil, M. d'Indy, to be exact, magisterially carrying on his master's tradition in the *Symphonie sur un thème montagnard*, where the piano expresses very perfectly the feeling of lofty poetry. Besides, M. d'Indy forgets his own work in attributing to Franck the sole initiative of so prolific a cause. He forgets his own *Poème des Montagnes*, which dates from 1881, and Alexis de Castillon's fine Concerto which, at its first performance in 1872, so lacerated Pasdeloup's dilettante audiences, whose ears were still buzzing with the empty banalities of the second empire, that the pianist—who was Saint-Saëns—was hissed off the platform without finishing it.

He forgets others too in France who at the same time were working for the same ends. Saint-Saëns, for instance, who did magnificent work at this juncture of our musical history; since 1858 he had enriched the repertoire of pianists by several concertos, the least of which is to-day an object of grateful admiration to musicians as well as to pianists; Lalo, whose unjustly discarded Concerto was full of broad dramatic inspiration; Fauré, then young Gabriel

César Franck

Fauré, whose refined and tender Ballade was finished in 1880; and Chabrier, in whose concentrated talent was the germ of all the picturesque French music of the generation that followed.

There was still another: Charles-Valentin Alkan, an organist by profession, who was interested in the piano and its resources, composer of music half good, half deplorable; he had worked unceasingly in the shadow of an insignificant career, known to very few, but worthy to be remembered for his influence on Franck, whom, I believe, he several times advised. Franck thought highly of his piano compositions, and in their best moments they bear a relation in style and method to certain passages in the *Djinns*, the work with which the composer of the *Béatitudes* was to open his new series for the piano.[1]

The reader must not imagine that I have any idea, in the foregoing pages, of making light of the historic significance of Franck's return to piano music, of discounting the value of it, or of underestimating the importance of its effect on the music that succeeded it. I am only trying to show that his motive and his intentions were shared by a few of his contemporaries, and those not the least.

It was with the *Djinns*, written in 1883—not 1884, as some commentators say—that Franck came back to the piano; and for four years, that is, till 1887, he

[1] The series of pieces by Alkan that Franck transcribed for the organ in 1889 is not without interest. They show, too, a singular resemblance of feeling with the transcriber's own work.

touched no other medium for the expression of his musical thought. We can, really, consider the piano part of the glorious Sonata he wrote in 1886 as an additional indication of the trend of the moment; it is as significant a part of his pianistic thought as the works that are wholly dedicated to the instrument of his choice.

At the most, he added a bar or two, from time to time, to the score of *Hulda*, begun in 1882, and made notes of the principal themes on which the Symphony in D minor is built.

The sub-title of 'symphonic poem' that Franck appended to his first work for piano and orchestra suggests that he had in mind Hugo's poem of the same name. (We can call it his first work—seeing that, on his own saying, the piano compositions he wrote previously are not to be included.) We shall find in it a sort of free interpretation of the legendary character of the *Djinns* in the Oriental fable, only occasionally bearing on the actual musical development.

Hugo's verses, made famous by his graphic style, have an underlying rhythm not unlike the plan of Franck's work. Both tone poem and verse are alike founded on a progressive extension of the cadence, to which a development of accumulated intensity corresponds. Then once the climax is reached—expressed in the release of longer sustained phrases—from this point, both in text and music, an exactly inverse order is instituted, working in a continuous diminuendo to the total disappearance of both words and music.

César Franck

But the impression which is evoked by the musical text is unquestionably an emotional one, while the verses only aspire to descriptive literary virtuosity; they are, besides, a little burdened by the arbitrary metre imposed upon them by the poet's caprice.

To start off with, the Thousand and One Nights tell us in the story of the *Djinns* that they are familiar spirits, half-way between angels and demons, some well-intentioned towards man, good servants of Islam, the guardians of the wise and virtuous; others evil and cruel genii, infidels. With a little expansion and the least flavour of drama embodied in the musical expression of each of these naïvely contrasted figures, there is, ready-made, a picturesque fancy quite rich enough in possibilities to stir the imagination of Franck, who often made use of weaker ideas than this.

If now we visualize the transposition of the fable to moral, even to Christian ends, and take the *Djinns* as symbolical of our worse instincts and desires, as the incarnation of evil, and imagine the human soul tormented and harassed by continual temptations, defending itself by heartfelt supplication, we shall grasp what Franck seems to have meant us to read into it, judging by the various expression indications in the piano score. Such a conception offered him the description of the struggle between good and evil ending in the tranquil victory of the good—so we gather from the last bars of the score—and the idea was too congenial for him to refrain from choosing it, under cover of a picturesque title which at least gives us some idea of its meaning, if it does not reveal the whole conception.

Moreover, the music of the *Djinns* has a particular interest for other reasons than the track of an idea which can be ignored without our being any less sensitive to the beauty of the work which it inspired.

In choosing the form of symphonic poem for piano and orchestra with the piano used as an instrument in dialogue with the others, and not as a solo instrument with an accompaniment, Franck discloses at the same time his wish to subordinate the piano to the music and to put virtuosity in its proper place. It was not that he was afraid of using it; he often does, and in the *Djinns* too; but while allowing that it was a part of the piano's particular function, he did not intend it to prejudice the natural development of the musical language, to involve unnecessary decoration, nor to try to gild barren ideas.

In this conception of the part played by the solo instrument Franck was anticipated among French composers, to my knowledge, only by Berlioz, who wrote a predominating part in *Harold in Italy* for the viola, but in a way that did not force the orchestra into the unworthy subordination that the concerto form so often entails.

In this I am glad to find myself in perfect agreement with M. d'Indy, and to be able to hail with him the importance of this readjustment of values, the interest of its impact on contemporary music, and thus on the mind of the public and on interpretative musicians. Among the striking works which derived directly from the instrumental aesthetic of the *Djinns*, I am able to cite a work of M. Vincent

César Franck

d'Indy, this *Symphonie sur un thème montagnard* which
I have already mentioned, undoubtedly the most
perfect and convincing proof of the excellence of
this method. I would also suggest Scriabin's *Pro-
metheus*, Richard Strauss's *Burlesque*, Debussy's *Fantaisie*, and nearer to our time, the *Fantaisie* of Fauré,
M. Witkowski's piece called *Mon Lac*, and the three
nocturnes of Manuel de Falla entitled *Nuits dans
les jardins d'Espagne*.

I have, I am afraid, given a very incomplete
picture of the revelations of a musical activity which
extended over more than forty years. But it is
enough to show the merit of Franck's conception of
music, and the nature of its consequences, in spite
of the diversity of style and influence which formed
it. In forcing the virtuoso out of his dominant
position, music resumes her position in the fore-
ground.

The *Djinns* offers few notable peculiarities from the
point of view of construction. As I have already
indicated by the comments on the probable subject
of the work, everything rests on the contrast of two
ideas—one rhythmic, dominating, almost aggressive;
the other melodic, emerging from unrest and even
anguish to the confident tranquillity of the answered
prayer. The orchestra first states in a lively duple
time a sort of fantastic scherzo to a muffled beat
jerked out by bass *pizzicati*; out of it flows a restless
melody hurrying through the harmonies in wild
contortions.

Several bars abruptly accented, more martial than
demoniacal, cut by a lightning zigzag from the piano,

lead to the presentation of the principal theme in the form of a dialogue between the solo instrument and the orchestra, in authoritative tones, not unlike the choir of the first Béatitude singing exultantly of the intoxication of power.

The tone fades and the second subject makes its appearance on the piano, at first in an eddy of restless distress, then flowing uneasily in a long chromatic descent whose intensity is still further heightened by the contrast of a whirling accompaniment that draws it into a tornado of sound. An almost classical development of basic themes opens at the striking change to a triple time, at once stormy and profound; its sonorous breadth rises against the clash of the first cadence, evoked a moment before by a rising crescendo.

Here there is a finely tempered passage for the piano, supported by the murmur of a quartet accompaniment presently broken by an uneasy recall of the introductory motif; the piano pours out its soul in ecstasy, leading us gradually from fear to hope, as Franck's expression marks, of which I have spoken, suggest, giving us the key to the interpretation of this passage. He first indicates: 'In the mood of prayer, but with a certain uneasy agitation,' then at the point where the eight-bar passage extends its lyrical flight and the orchestra is silent: 'With gradually increasing tranquillity and confidence.'

Here there is certainly a moment of expressive, ecstatic intensity, illuminated, as by a ray of peace, by an unexpected modulation from the minor to the major, which creates an atmosphere of limpid contemplation in which the restless agony of the opening passage is quietly absorbed.

This short relaxation is troubled afresh by the rhythmic interruption of the battalion of introductory themes, accompanied this time by a mocking outburst of clarinets. And then the repetition of almost the whole of the first development; in spite of the liberties which his choice of subject seemed to invite, Franck here moves in the most classical of musical conventions, even including the strict return to the tonic for the recapitulation of the second subject.

Towards the end, however, he brings in an important change of feeling which relates it, as I have already remarked, to Hugo's verses. Instead of the original crescendo, it is a diminuendo that leads on to the peroration, in which the triple-time passage which was the essential climax of the music's growth recurs in contraction and shorn of its emotional meaning. And the flying rush of piano arpeggios that come to rest again on the regained serenity of conclusive major chords finally dispel the nightmare hallucination, and it fades once more into the void.

This seems to me to be the correct reading of César Franck's symphonic poem, as one strains to decipher behind the music the meaning of a missing text; and one recognizes at once why there is a certain incongruity between it and the composer's musical temperament.

In a prejudiced and unsympathetic criticism of Franck that I shall refer to again later, Camille

Saint-Saëns makes a remark that is not without justice in spite of his bias against him: 'Berlioz was more artist than musician; Franck was more musician than artist. He was no poet, and a sense of the picturesque is entirely lacking in his music.' The comment is a little curt, and it also raises the question whether all poetry is faced with this strange dilemma, to be picturesque—or nothing. But without doubt this is the blind spot in Franck's genius, and in embarking on a subject which involved him in the musical expression of the fantastic and the demoniacal, he was bound to fall short in realization. Even for the most rhapsodic and fanciful of descriptions Franck was incapable of moving outside the rigours of musical forms, those stern classical laws of construction to which both by instinct and education he traced the essence of music's strength.

I have it on reliable authority that he had reached the point where he had fixed in advance the modulatory scheme of his next work, regardless of what form it might take. Masterpieces like the symphony, the quartet, and the chorales were founded on an idealized scheme of this sort, in which anxiety for harmonic balance preceded the actual rhythmic or melodic inspiration. I do not wish to start a critical discussion of his method; the results of it are there, eloquent and conclusive enough, in spite of Saint-Saëns's opinion. But so singular a faculty must have its weaker side; and if the passages in the *Djinns* that one can term religious profit by a disposition closely akin to their emotional quality, by contrast, the passages devoted to the descriptions of the fantastic—in fact, those which should give the work its character—lack the force and originality of thought and expression necessary to complete success; but nevertheless, the work is still striking in its detail.

The pianistic writing is indeed of the most novel and sustained interest, if we consider the period and compare it with the concert pieces of contemporary date, especially in its relations between the piano and the orchestra. Nowhere do we meet the least trace of the declamatory style and the empty stretches of virtuosity with which the genre is inevitably associated. The piano is merged into the flow of the music without trying to focus our attention, without burdening its movement and without interrupting its logical development, simply adding to the orchestra the resource of a broad and lyrical tone, enriching it with an added timbre; it joins with infinite flexibility in the ebb and flow of feeling, altering as occasion demands the character of its technique to underline the better a specially significant passage, passing easily and naturally from the ironic vivacity of a turn or an arpeggio to the expressive rounding of a melodic phrase.

I have spoken of the unusual beauty of that passage where the melody, given out unharmonized by the piano, floats above the plastic base of tremolo strings. In the later pages the emotional tremolo that previously supported the melody is replaced simply by a series of repeated chords, suddenly transforming its character, giving birth to a sort of confident exaltation. Certain passages in the piano part of the quintet had already suggested a similar sentiment, and by a similar technical device. Again, further on we hear it in the tranquil radiance of crystalline triplet quavers in the upper octaves of the piano, as they shed a moonlit peace over the sombre dying chords in the orchestra. And yet again, in the final recapitulation in the tonic, when the rapid point of a chromatic figure engraves a fine pattern into the tonal solidity of an expressive dialogue between the solo instrument and the orchestra.

Other instances disclose the happy association of the expressive medium and the descriptive sentiment of the work. It is unnecessary to stress the point, because the careful reader cannot misunderstand the character of these details, nor mistake the kind of technique they need.

I should like to point out, at the same time, that Franck's piano technique needs a special study of legato in relation to the expressive demands of the polyphonic style—not only as far as the piano technique of the *Djinns* is concerned but also in a more general sense. His pupils have over and over again attested to the extraordinary capacity of his hands for big stretches, and Mme Rongier's faithful portrait of him at the organ reproduces this slightly abnormal physical characteristic, which enabled him to compass a twelfth easily. It is a peculiarity which could not fail to influence his instrumental style, and it is in most cases the real practical difficulty—I would say the only one—in his work.

César Franck

The *Djinns* was dedicated to Mme de Serres, who had had as a girl, under the name of Caroline Montigny-Rémaury, a well-earned success as a pianist. Franck himself wrote the transcription for two pianos which was published by Enoch of Paris in the Collection Litolff on 15 February 1884, ten years before the publication of the orchestral score.

The first performance of the version for orchestra took place on 15 March 1885, at the Châtelet, under the baton of Édouard Colonne, with Louis Diémer at the piano, in the course of a concert at which the first part of the programme was devoted to the following works introduced by the Société Nationale de Musique: *Symphony in D Minor* by Gabriel Fauré, the *Djinns*, an *Orientale* for orchestra by Claudius Blanc, and the *Rapsodie d'Auvergne* by Saint-Saëns. In the account of this concert *L'Art Musical* of 31 March does not even mention Franck's work and reserves its enthusiasm for the *Rapsodie d'Auvergne*, which, moreover, it miscalls the *Rapsodie Auvergnate*, and for Diémer's brilliant performance. On the other hand the *Ménestrel*, over the signature of G. Mersac, publishes the following critique, which Franck must have held very dear, unused as he was to such expressions of appreciation:

'M. L. Diémer gave a distinguished performance of the piano part in a symphonic poem by M. César Franck, the *Djinns*, interesting work that it was for the direct originality of its thought and the admirable polish of style. As I listened to the fine logic of these developments and the arresting effects of the blending of the piano with the orchestra, I was struck by the thought of how sad it is that the name of this eminent musician is so rarely seen on programmes, too little honoured at a time when he is one of the masters of our epoch, and will indubitably remain one.'[1]

In his essays on Pascal and Leonardo da Vinci, Paul Valéry several times deprecates the motive that allows us to confuse the actual man who creates a work of art with the man suggested by that work of art. He maintains that in the very intellectual process that urges us to infer the man behind the idea there is an element that leads almost inevitably to distortion.

I do not know if the author of the *Architecte* extends this suspicious attitude to the works of musical art—'faithless music' as he somewhere stigmatizes it. But if it should be so, I suggest to him the *Prélude, Choral et Fugue* as an example of the amazing truthfulness with which an art can mirror the essentials of personality and even of character— and an art fleeting and intangible, too, the only thing capable of expressing the inexpressible, as Goethe described it. There are few musical works, indeed, through which one can so clearly divine the man

---

[1] The public reception was no more than polite, and as much addressed to the pianist as to the composer. But Franck was always prone to think the least demonstration of approval as in excess of its merits, and was the first to attribute this modest success to Diémer's performance. He went up to him in the foyer of the Châtelet to congratulate him as soon as the concert was over, and promised to show his gratitude by dedicating a small work to him. The 'small work' in question was to be the *Variations symphoniques*.

behind the artist. Running quickly through the more obvious instances that continue to endure through the centuries, I might name the *Stabat Mater* of Palestrina, a Dialogue of Schütz, the *Chromatic Fantasia* of Bach, or the poignant *Passion according to S. John,* which was undoubtedly nearer to the heart of Cantor of Leipzig than the more beautiful *Passion according to S. Matthew,* the *Requiem* of Mozart, the thirteenth Quartet or the Sonata Op. 110 of Beethoven, the *Fantaisie* of Schumann, a Ballade or a Nocturne of Chopin. This is music that describes its composers better, with more moving sincerity and with keener insight, than the most life-like of portraits or the most meticulous of biographies. If any one is anxious to create for himself a true picture of Franck, to penetrate the warm simplicity of his beliefs, to understand his spirit, luminous and yet naïve, contemplative and yet zealous, to realize the confident certainty and the generous breadth of his faith—more an inspiration than a doctrine, as some one happily said—he has only to turn to this inimitable masterpiece and examine the grave harmony of its development. There he will find the 'direct reflection, the natural extension, and the perfect expression of the mind that conceived it and brought it to birth'.

Franck's initial idea in sketching out the plan of the work which was destined to be his most important piano composition both in substance and style, was, as we know, to remind musicians of the classical form of the Prelude and Fugue, rather neglected since the fine works that Mendelssohn produced in the genre. He wished in this way to show that the old logical basis, on which a whole world of music had grown up during nearly two hundred years, had lost none of its merits; that the contemporary method of expression could fit into its mould without sacrificing a tithe of its recent technical resources, and that only a pedantic academicism had hardened it into a school exercise.

It was not till later, and as he got on with the work, M. d'Indy tells us, that he had the idea of binding the Prelude and the Fugue with a Choral whose melodic nature should dominate the whole piece. It was a stroke of genius, softening and humanizing a form naturally austere, investing it, without taking from its inherent dignity, with the emotional power and vibrant inner feeling by which Franck's work establishes its irresistible ascendancy over us.

Johann Sebastian Bach seems to have foreseen every future musical resource; he had already hinted at the need for a balance of expression which should bind his Preludes or his Toccatas with the Fugues they preceded, whether by a calculated contrast of rhythms and movements which were to prove complementary, or, on the other hand, by a marked similarity of character. And in adopting this unifying principle in his work Franck would only have been developing a previous conception; but he added this new innovation, prolific in results—the use of a single basic theme common to all three parts; and then, with the Choral, a second melody of different feeling, which answers the original cyclic theme, or imposes itself upon it.

César Franck

By setting forth two ideas in a form hitherto based strictly on one—naturally the double Fugue is an exception, but it proceeds from an entirely different basis—Franck thus introduces an element of poetic contrast like that which creates the dramatic course of the Sonata or of the Symphony.

I could not make a better nor more concise analysis of the *Prélude, Choral et Fugue* than M. d'Indy's. It is as follows:

'The Prelude is cast in the classic mould of the old prelude in the suite. Its one theme is stated in the tonic, then in the dominant, and ends in the Beethoven manner with a phrase which completely rounds off the theme. The Choral, in three sections, alternates between E flat and C minor, composed of two distinct elements: a superbly expressive motif which heralds and prepares the subject of the coming Fugue, and the Choral proper, whose three prophetic phrases roll out with tranquil grandeur in sonorous curves. After an episode which takes us from E flat minor to the principal key of B minor, the Fugue opens its successive expositions; after their development the melody and rhythm of the complementary theme of the Prelude returns; the rhythm persists in accompaniment of an animated restatement of the Choral theme; then soon after, the Fugue subject itself enters in the principal key, in a manner that unites the three elements of the work in a sublime peroration.'

Less generously inspired is Saint-Saëns's comment on Franck's composition in a captious little work entitled *Les Idées de M. Vincent d'Indy*; I have already cited one extract in speaking of the *Djinns*; here is the reference to the present piece:

'. . . A work . . . uncouth, and tiresome to play, in

which the chorale is no chorale, and the fugue no fugue, for it breaks down as soon as the exposition is over and wanders on through endless digressions which are no more like a fugue than a mollusc is like a mammal, and which are a dear price to pay for a brilliant peroration.'

'Uncouth and tiresome' though it may be, the execution of the *Prélude, Choral et Fugue* none the less opens out to the pianist who undertakes it a vast field of highly interesting problems. They have as much to do with its underlying sentiment and the exact shades of expression necessary to it, as with the technical difficulties it sets up. A serious pianist would never be satisfied only to give what one might call a broadly architectural reading; otherwise he would be grossly misunderstanding what constitutes the novel beauty of this work.

Franck never considered that element in a work which we call form in any other light than as the physical body of the essential work of art, meant to serve as the tangible outward form clothing the idea, which he himself described as the soul of the music. But this conception is rather in danger of giving rise to exaggeratedly sentimental interpretations, especially in a generation of pianists who tend to read music through the eyes of a temperament over-excited by the continual study of romantic works. A great contemporary artist, Mlle Blanche Selva, who has devoted a large part of her interest and talent to the interpretation of Franck's works, once remarked with perfect truth that Franck's rhythmic fluctuations are quite distinct from *rubato*, and that they are born not of fancy but of emotion. Indeed, Franck's lyrical vein, broad and free as it is, has not that personal, intimate touch which releases the rare abandon of Chopin or Schumann. It is objective, sustained by a strong sense of tradition, and inclines rather to generalize the emotion that impels it.

The many passages, principally in the Prelude and in the episode which links the Choral to the Fugue, which are marked to be played with a certain freedom, are, therefore, not to be given too personal an interpretation, or too marked an emotional licence. They are an integral part of the work whose close unity I have just stressed. One disproportionate outburst of emotional feeling—and the ideal curve that encompasses the whole piece is spoilt. This fine point holds a danger as formidable as any uncomprehending rigidity could be. But if the feeling of these passages is genuinely sought and expressed in interpretation as a lofty aspiration towards the eternal and divine; if that mournful cantilena, the organic cell and essential theme of the work, which twice reiterates its plaint in the Prelude, is made to convey the tremulous eagerness of questioning hope—as it unconsciously returns to the initial tempo in the four bars which follow; if, in the episode, the pauses which cut through the tentative forecasts of the Fugue are instilled with sad and troubled foreboding, without too apparent an effect, then the rhythmic freedom that Franck hoped for will follow a perfect course, and the idea will truly become the soul of the music, as he affirmed.

In playing the superb Choral, on the other hand, there is no ambiguity possible. Its character is obvious after a first reading; in the simplicity of the moving dialogue between the two symmetrically alternating phrases which form its base. The symbolical meaning of it can thus be accurately read without any possibility of distorting Franck's own thought: a first phrase in march rhythm, characterized by a melodic quaver figure, plaintively chromatic, punctuated with syncopations, and breathing a sentiment of unwearying supplication—the eternal quest of humanity for justice and consolation. Then the response of the second phrase sounded three times, emerging from veiled revelation to luminous certainty; this bears an almost immobile rhythm of crotchets in massed diatonic harmonies, through which the Godhead speaks. It is an overwhelmingly eloquent expression of the *cri du cœur* in 'Polyeucte': 'Je vois, je sais, je crois, je suis désabusée.'

The fine Fugue with which Franck crowns his masterpiece for the piano is foreshadowed in Mendelssohn's great Fugue in E minor, written by the side of his dying friend; in the overture to his oratorio *Elijah* where a sentiment of urgent supplication is expressed solely through the fugato form; again, in the opening of Liszt's Variations on 'Weinen, Klagen', and in the passage in the *Dante Symphony* which portrays the agonized torment of souls struggling in purgatory.

It is only to the point to cite one instance of the form from Beethoven's pen; for from the time when he created the Mass in D, that shattering and superhuman profession of faith, he was so irresistibly attracted by the inner richness of a style which perfectly reflected his own need of abstract and condensed philosophical expression, that there is no work of his at all, after that date, which does not incorporate it; but the fugue which concludes Op. 110, cut poignantly by the strangled sob of the Arioso dolente, evokes, like Franck's fugue, the feeling that it emanates from a spiritual urgency rather than from a principle of musical style.

Nevertheless, though the finale of the *Prélude, Choral et Fugue* can be emotionally identified with these other great examples of the expressive capacity of the fugue form, the reasoned independence of its construction frees it from any stigma of imitation or assimilation of other ideas. Saint-Saëns quite rightly said, though in blind misunderstanding of it: 'This fugue is no fugue.' The exposition, the successive entries of the four parts are, undoubtedly, conventionally strict, and the ensuing development is inspired by the most correct models in the genre. But all the time in the inner murmur of the music one is conscious that even the fugue subject does not contain within itself its own impulse and its own end, that it has its being in a world of such contrite anguish that some external intervention must be invoked to relieve it from its pain. And so, after the appearance of the quaver triplets which increase its restlessness, and the climax of the crescendo which sweeps up to a paroxysm of agony and entreaty, the theme of the Choral re-enters, gentle solace amid the liquid trembling of celestial harps; and we, who have just witnessed that intolerable pain, experience such relief and regained calm that the tumult of triumphant voices proclaiming the Word in the peroration seems like the release of our own emotional tension.

Here, indeed, is a consequence that no treatise on counterpoint, nor the over-academic musicians, could calculate on. But then they are not supposed to take genius into account; and it is genius of the purest imaginable that inspired this sublime work of art, grave and lofty expression of a Christian spirit longing for his God, which by the very glory of its music convinces us of a universal plan, and turns the pathetic echo of human desires and aspirations towards a glorious ideal.

The *Prélude, Choral et Fugue* was published in 1884, at the same time as the *Djinns*, in the Collection Litolff by Enoch. It was dedicated to Mlle Marie Poitevin, afterwards Mme G. Hainl, who played it at its first performance at the Salle Pleyel, at a concert of the Société Nationale de Musique on 25 January 1885. But the manuscript, recently offered in homage to Her Majesty the Queen of the Belgians, shows marks of erasure on the dedicatory page which might lead one to suppose that this name was not the first in the composer's mind.[1]

The more recent editions have removed a fault which persisted in all the earlier issues for nearly forty years, and I must refer to it here. In the last bar but one of the Choral, the last quaver is an F in

[1] I share M. d'Indy's view, however, that the work was written specially for Mlle Poitevin.

the G clef which the presence of a flat to a preceding F—the F is the second quaver of the same bar—supposes to be altered by the same accidental.

A copy that Franck corrected, of which I am the privileged possessor, has long made it possible for me to point out this mistake. The last F is natural and is linked by the interval of a major second and not a minor second to the E flat which ends the Choral.

There are some works which one takes to one's heart, just as one does some people. One hesitates to analyse 'love at first sight' in the fear that too profound an examination may cause disillusionment. And such was my state of mind when I undertook, for this hastily promised study, the analysis of the work of Franck's that I have played most, and of which I have had the pleasure of being at least a loving interpreter—if I had no other merit—in nearly every city in the old and the new worlds.

The *Variations symphoniques* made their first, irresistible impression on me as a young disciple of Louis Diémer, to whom the work is dedicated, one day when he asked me to play over the orchestral part at sight on a second piano as an impromptu rehearsal. At that moment a new musical horizon spread out before my gaze, limited up till then, by the rigour (no doubt salutary enough) of my studies, to less noble productions of concerted music; and I did not relax my efforts till my master yielded to my wish and allowed me to work at the solo part of the work he had just brought to my notice.

It is without even having dreamt of going back on

this first impression, this sudden and total capitulation, that for a number of years I have tried in my turn to communicate to others the work that has fascinated me. And in these circumstances to discuss a work so rooted in my affection, to attempt to fathom and then to describe its beauties, was to risk destroying a cherished enchantment, to risk watching a secret loveliness fade which had coloured my whole career; in a way it was like trying, as a child would, to prise open my affection to see what was inside.

I have come away from this attempt with my instinctive feeling revived, fortified in my devotion, happy to be able to discount as false that otherwise charming aphorism of an eighteenth-century author —that it is a poor love that can say why it loves. If the *Variations symphoniques* do not exhibit so forceful an ideal as the *Prélude, Choral et Fugue*, or the quartet, or the first movement of the symphony, it unquestionably is, with the sonata for piano and violin, the most perfect artistic production that Franck wrote. I do not say the most beautiful, but the most lucid and the most polished.

Here the balance and proportion are admirably adjusted; the piano part is conceived in relation to the orchestra with so rare an understanding of its resources and care for its limitation, the blending or the clash of timbres is so spontaneously achieved, and with so assured a touch, that as the work sweeps on the listener is convinced that the music written there has found not only its happiest medium in the combination of piano and orchestra, but its only possible medium.

César Franck

Obviously such a statement only refers to the perfection of Franck's method of expressing his musical inspiration. A closer examination will show us the unique quality of this inspiration.

The principle of variation was the first and most natural manifestation of musical ornament, at least as far as instrumental music is concerned. Before the development or recapitulation of themes, the stimulating return of their rhythm, and the variety and colour of their modulations, had come to enrich the course of the music with their satisfying logic, the simplest way of renewing a musical theme was to surround it with devices of grace-notes and diminutions which nevertheless were scrupulously careful to preserve the original line of the theme. For, as Sebastian de Brossard advises in his *Dictionnaire de Musique*, the first work of this kind, one should 'always be able to recognize the underlying Air, that we call the Simple, through these adornments, as it were, which some call Broderies'.

Indifferent as he was, as we know, to the way instrumental music manifested itself, J.-J. Rousseau set himself at the end of the eighteenth century to reproduce Brossard's definition and advice. It is according to the system of repetition and added ornament that the clavichordists called the 'double', and which were similarly applied in Chaconnes and Passacaglias, but then limited more narrowly to the movement of the bass, that countless airs and variations were written during several centuries.

It was a music full of 'industry and rule', as a seventeenth-century theorist already gloomily observed;

a method which by its very simplicity could only too easily degenerate into a conventional formula; and so far from extending the diverse qualities which existed in the original theme, it tended on the contrary to devitalize it, exhausting its substance, while engendering a tonal and rhythmic monotony that the most versatile of grace-notes, the most florid and charming of decoration did not always succeed in hiding.

Once more we must look in the work of J. S. Bach for the violation of method by which genius frees and transfigures it; the thirty variations for the clavecin with two manuals, known under the name of the Goldberg Variations, put into practice, with calm audacity, the satisfying resources of an enlivening counterpoint. Though they do not yet ruthlessly break away from the principles of the form as we have just seen it defined by Brossard and Rousseau, at least they anticipate and pave the way for the mighty Thirty-three Variations on a theme of Diabelli which Beethoven was to throw down as a challenge at the feet of his contemporaries a century later, or the *Études symphoniques* in the form of Variations, that Schumann once thought of calling *Variations pathétiques* to indicate their meaning and compass. All these are broad, free constructions, full of passionate inventiveness, novelty, fine licence; the theme has long ceased to be the essential, central point of the work, and appears a kind of mere thematic excuse for it, as each variation tends more and more to rule it out in favour of newer and more fertile schemes. Franck was to go still farther than his famous predecessors in this direction, and the *Variations symphoniques* contain profoundly important modifications to the sacrosanct tradition, as much in its basis as in its method.

In its basis, by the choice of a theme with a double subject, of which each phrase is the foundation of its own separate development, and creates through the work the conflict of two expressive cross-currents by which it is enriched and made productive. In its method, by the blending of the orchestra and the piano, an inestimable extension of colour and variety, and by doing away with the set division between the variations, whose unvarying squareness gives place to the flexibility of an organic whole made perfectly plastic and unified.

Actually, Liszt had already suggested the possibilities of such a conception in his Variations on the *Dies Irae*, under the title of *Totentanz*, but without having quite freed himself from the constraint of formalism.

At the beginning of the *Variations symphoniques* Franck sets forth the clash between the two elements of his theme under pretext of an introduction: an almost aggressively vigorous rhythm for the strings answered by an appealing melody for the piano. At once the general feeling of the piece is established, calculated to appeal rather to the emotions than to the intellect. Thanks to this opening conflict of mood —a legacy from the Beethoven method—which is the vital principle of the work, Franck at once creates a dramatic situation where we are to see these two elements in turn opposed or fused, clashing or merging, without losing anything of their initial character.

It is a fine opening, displaying to us the protagonists of an impassioned struggle, where we might have expected merely pleasantly ingenious devices. Here is a fresh revelation of the powerful inventive gift aptly described by a quotation from Franck's beloved Grétry: 'It is only the man accustomed to the discipline of rules who is now and then allowed to break them, because he alone knows that in a similar case the rule did not hold good.'

Let us follow out the course of this generative theme and observe its impact on the work. After the few introductory bars of dialogue I have already referred to, the strings, *pizzicato*, introduce the subject in triple time as, several pages later, it is given by the piano. Here it is only outlined and separated from its complete exposition section by a sustained recitativo passage in four-time by the solo instrument, forming an expressive commentary on the second element of the introduction.

The opening note of conflict is revived by an orchestral crescendo, preparing an episode where, like Orpheus trying to assuage the anger of the Furies, the piano in passionate entreaty crashes against the inexorable answer of a savage unison for the strings, thrice repeated. But, like the guardians of Hell in the myth, the strings relent at last before the persuasive, throbbing insistence of the melody, and a train of infinitely delicate and subtle modulations leads us now to the proper exposition of the theme, exquisitely given by the piano in a mood of profound melancholy. Here the two elements, hitherto only heard in opposition, merge together and unite in an atmosphere of consolation and tenderness.

The two linked variations which follow are perfectly wedded to the melodic line of the subject thus described, and stress the mood of reconciliation, while working imperceptibly towards a stately modulation to D major, which marshals the forces of the orchestra on a new, luminous, and rhythmic statement of the theme. The piano shares in this animation, underlining its melody in octaves, and joins a rush of passionate aspiration which now and then attains heroic dimensions. Then the rhythm dies down, the tone fades, and the deep sonorous note of the 'cellos states the theme, which up to the opening of the finale acts as a ground-bass beneath an ecstatic murmur of semiquavers on the solo instrument. It is a mood of ineffable contemplation, a moment as it were of arrested time, which releases in the listener a nameless, irresistible urgency: whether of grief or hope, of tears or tenderness, one does not know.

'From whence, oh my God, comes this peace that floods my soul?' cries the poet, led by such an ecstasy to the very gate of mystery and revelation. In all music I know few pages to be compared with these. There does not exist in all Franck's work, even in the compositions essentially religious, the expression of a nobler mood.

In the same way that Beethoven opens the magnificent peroration of the variations in the 'Archduke' Trio by the deliberate snap of a commonplace chord of the seventh, which drops us back from the sublime to the finite with a jerk, so Franck brings us back to earth after the episode just described by the simplest but most effective of modulatory devices.

Following a chromatic motif on the piano, which vanishes in the vague harmonies sustained on the strings, an ordinary undisguised dominant trill passes from the minor to the major, effects an entire change of mood, and creates an impression of vivacity which persists from this moment to the end of the work. The woodwind engages with a lively rhythm, soon accented by alternating piano chords, on a new fragmentary version of the first element of the theme, the active element, while the lower strings secure the second, or expressive, element, which they give out with conscious optimism, with joyous bounding sweeps of the bow. From now onwards, this final variation, most diverse of them all, moves in a continual atmosphere of happy animation.

Even the most convinced of Franck enthusiasts have criticized in all good faith the suddenness of this transition, and regretted that the theme in its reappearance seems so little in keeping with the preceding pages. Critics have deplored the rhythmic banality of this passage and the harmonic commonplaces which—they say—are here disclosed.

But very far from causing disappointment or surprise, it seems to me that the candour and fresh spontaneity of the finale is an indispensable part of the general balance on which the work rests and to which I shall refer later. It seems to me that no other device would in the same way have ensured the variety and completed the mood of the piece,

founded as it is on an emotional progression. Moreover, while one may admit the momentary weakness
of several bars—at least in comparison with the
unusual fineness of the preceding episode—this
sudden metamorphosis of mood becomes the excuse
for wonderful new delights and an extraordinary
wealth of colour in the course of the ensuing
development. Recall the eloquent statement of the
octave motif when the piano embarks again on a sort
of recitative after the bars I have just mentioned;
study the ingenious brilliance of the lively triplet
movement which is displayed at the repetition of the
original theme, the wood-wind replaced this time by
the strings *pizzicato*; recognize the force and brilliance of the *divertissement* where the piano chords
answer the design of the basses as they give out the
theme; and you will find it possible to admit after all
that the 'commonplaces' of the new method that
Franck has employed for the last section of the work
by no means cramp its development; on the contrary
its development communicates a unique impulsive
force.

A short *tutti*, modulating noisily, leaves this first
section of the finale in suspense on two vigorous
chords; then the piano interposes a momentary
change of feeling and rhythm by introducing a
tender paraphrase, in triple time, of the second
element of the theme, in the hitherto unused key of
E flat major. The whimsical suppleness and delicately sensuous glow of this new note contrasts
with the characteristic prevailing freedom, and forms
a convenient means of bestowing really pointed

significance upon the return to the original duple time when the flute and later the violins reintroduce it subtly under the graceful ornamentation of the piano. The first half of the finale follows in the tonic key, according to classical formula, up to the triumphant conclusion of the most vigorous and varied work that Franck ever wrote for the piano.

This analysis is very incomplete. But I hope it enables the reader to see, in the series of variations, three separate lyrical moods whose succession moulds the development in the unified plan I have alluded to earlier. Each of them represents a group of variations of distinct character which can easily be defined. The first is exquisitely expressive in atmosphere and takes us, as an introduction, as far as the complete exposition of the theme for the piano, that is, to the *Allegretto quasi andante*. The second, the real kernel of the variations proper, stretches from here as far as the finale, twisting among eloquent key changes, and passing from tender tranquillity to a vein of devout contemplation, after having been tinged with vivacity. The third includes the finale whose note of convincing perfect joy I have just described. In my opinion the interest and quality of its performance depends necessarily on the emotional and intellectual interpretation of these three main divisions; soloist and conductor must aim at making this expressive and logical construction clearly perceptible. For, as with the *Djinns*, and here still more, however important the role of pianist may be, he can only express it through an intimate collaboration with the orchestra; for in these two works was bridged the gulf which at one period and in one style had seemed to separate virtuosity from music.

It was nevertheless not that he discarded any of the resources of piano technique in the *Variations symphoniques*, for there are many places in the score which offer an opportunity for showing off technique, and in a most fascinating way. And at the risk of repeating myself, I cannot resist the temptation to go back over the various passages in the piano part, where the fine writing is a singularly perfect channel for the beauty of the musical idea flowing through it.

First, I would emphasize the felicitous disposition of instruments in the first half-dozen bars where the piano's appealing tones are set against the crabbed accents of the strings.

In the *Adagio* of the Concerto in G Beethoven reversed the traditional roles in the same way, assigning to the percussive instrument the soft curve of pathetic melody, and opposing to it a menacing rhythmic attack from the bowed instruments. The purpose and execution are too strikingly similar, indeed, for it to be the result of a chance resemblance. But such a model would have proved inimitable for any one but Franck; and the resemblance here is in no sense a mere copy, because one feels that the procedure is necessitated by imperious emotional exigencies, and also because the new method reveals a wide sincerity.

Then there is the broad recitative passage expanding the original theme in which the octaves in the upper part acquire a force unexpected in this register of the piano, thanks to the eddying vibrations of the accompaniment, sustained and prolonged by a liberal use of the pedal. Again, immediately after the exposition of the theme in its triple rhythm, there is the tonal dialogue between the solo instrument and the strings, tender and melancholy, a pure intimacy of melody unimpaired by the exchange of timbres, and only varied, without being disturbed, by the clear hard progression of chords on the piano, above the 'cello theme, in the next variation.

Yet another passage is where the ripple of rising chromatic thirds is played with nervous force by the thumbs of both hands, as a flutter of semiquavers enlivens the pace of the whole. And later, where the expressive sextuplet movement, almost in Schumann's manner, accompanies the meditative recapitulation of the theme, heard on the 'cellos, in a continual oscillation between major and minor.

Finally, there is the calm, ineffable peace of those arpeggios divided between the two hands, whose tone dies away as obscure modulations draw them upwards to the higher reaches of the piano, seeming to lose them at last in unattainable distance.

I have already called attention to the individual character of most of the pianistic combinations of the finale; I only need go back to remark on the technical skill of the intermediate passage in E flat, in which the thread of a persuasive motif is woven delicately into the filmy web of quavers.

It goes without saying that on hearing the work none of these details count for themselves, and that their special interest is entirely subject to the conception of the work as a whole. There is no place in the performance of a composition so perfectly grave and moral for the flourishes of virtuosity. But respect by no means implies a colourless, reticent interpretation, and truth seems to be able to combine dignity with initiative, and to demonstrate here both its logic and its sensibility.

The first performance of the *Variations symphoniques* took place at the Salle Pleyel on 1 May 1886 at the annual orchestral concert of the Société Nationale, with Louis Diémer as the soloist. Above the initials F. N., the *Ménestrel* of 9 May gives the following rather non-committal account of it: 'In this work, the theme is of fine freshness and delicate distinction, supported by all the craft of a fluent and mature technique.' On 30 January of the following year, Franck included it in a concert of his works organized at the Cirque d'hiver by his pupil's exertions.

The first half, under the direction of Pasdeloup, consisted of the *Chasseur maudit* and the *Variations symphoniques*; the second part of *Ruth* and the *airs de ballet* from *Hulda*. Franck afterwards conducted excerpts from the *Béatitudes*. By an unhappy chance, some say by a mistake of the leader, the orchestra made a wrong start which damaged the performance of the *Variations*, and they had to recommence the finale after an interruption. In the *Ménestrel* of 6 February 1887—this magazine was probably the only contemporary publication which recorded Franck's musical activities without extreme hostility —Doolmetsch speaks first of the *Chasseur maudit*, then adding: 'The *Variations symphoniques* for piano and orchestra followed, a work in which the piano seemed to me to play rather a subordinate role in spite of all the brilliance used by its excellent interpreter, M. Louis Diémer.' This, actually, creates a slightly contradictory impression. But it moderates other excesses, which I have neither inclination nor space to quote, by this banal remark which reflects perfectly the average feeling of the public of that day—a public from which, alas, musicians themselves were not entirely excluded: 'Whether one appreciates the poetry of César Franck much or little, one must grant this composer a considerable skill, and at the same time an artistic integrity which is never impaired by the slightest seeking after commonplace effects.'

People have since come to think that there is something more than that in the work of this composer.

The *Variations symphoniques*, composed in 1885, were published by Enoch in March 1886, in the form of a transcription for two pianos. The orchestral version did not appear till February 1894.

As in the *Prélude, Choral et Fugue*, a fault still persists in the two-piano version. The left-hand trill in the solo part, at the beginning of the finale, should join the one in the right hand on the third bar of the C and not on the fifth.

From the same year, 1885, dates the composition of a *Danse lente* for the piano, meant for the Album du Gaulois, in which it appeared in 1886. It is a pleasant and skilful little piece which needs no other commentary.

* * *

César Franck

Many of Franck's pupils and interpreters still find it impossible to decide which they prefer, the *Prélude, Choral et Fugue* or the *Prélude, Aria et Finale*. Without wishing to impose my own opinion, and above all not valuing it above others except as a quite personal feeling, I will not disguise the fact that I prefer the first of these two works, disclosing as it does so singular a mating of inspiration and style.

In the *Prélude, Aria et Finale*, in spite of the sublime loveliness of certain passages, I cannot avoid a certain impression of conflict between the basic ideas of the work and its architectural construction. Franck's motive in writing his last piano composition—which is also the most important in actual size—was perfectly clear. He had in mind the regeneration of sonata form by the use of a cyclic method similar to that which engendered the emotional intensity of the Symphony in D minor.

But the themes of the symphony, by their contrasting types and their amazing flexibility, have for their development a wealth of resource in what one might call—to borrow a phrase from the drama —the musical situations of the work; and the underlying themes of the *Prélude, Aria et Finale*, on the contrary, seem by their very nature to gain nothing from a similar treatment.

Moreover, the exclusive use of duple rhythm for the three sections of the work results in melodic designs that are different in feeling being worked out in an almost identical scheme. There is an analogous case in Schumann's C major Fantasia, which carries the marks of a like constraint in spite of its emotional intensity. But the heady inexperience of youth excuses the young Leipzig student for disregarding a principle of composition which is both elementary and a matter of recognized tradition; there must be another explanation to account for its disregard in a work of maturity, full of wisdom and skill.

I can only find it, perhaps, in the preconceived wish to set the themes in juxtaposition without changing the rhythmic beat, which thus flows on unchanged to the moving conclusion of the Finale, where the previously separate subjects of the Prelude and the Aria reappear and merge into each other.

It may also be said in defence that the different sections of the *Prélude, Choral et Fugue* are also cast in the uniform beat of a four-time. Certainly, but these sections are musically cumulative, and only represent progressive states of an emotional life shared by the whole work; this is not the case with the *Prélude, Aria et Finale*, where each section has its distinct identity.

And finally, though it must be admitted that this is a purely personal feeling, I do not feel that the piano is, *par excellence*, the perfect instrument to interpret this last work that Franck devoted to it. In spite of the nobler austerity of subject in the *Prélude, Choral et Fugue*, we are continually amazed there at the exact blending of inspiration and expressive medium, at the fecundity of resource, and the felicity of writing for the instrument; in the *Prélude, Aria et Finale*, we sometimes find ourselves imagining an organ timbre or a string quartet as more

César Franck

exactly appropriate to express its melodic nature than the percussive instrument.

I need not point out how great an admiration and respect on my part accompanies these reserves of criticism, and were I not engaged in a comparative study I should express an unconditional and grateful surrender before this glorious work of Franck's genius. For the rest, the ensuing analysis will provide more reasons for enthusiasm than for criticism. They will dispense with the need for any further apology, even in the eyes of the most determined partisans of Franck's piano work.

There is a Piero della Francesca in the National Gallery showing a choir of angels singing with a radiantly vivid and reverent praise to the glory of the Babe of Bethlehem; it could serve as a perfect pictorial representation of the Prelude's first subject. Those sweet angel faces irradiate the same fervour and faith, the same joyous gratitude, as this serene melody, which moves in shining peace to the rhythm of a slow processional.

The exposition takes no less than forty-two bars, and is formed of three repetitions, with simple modifications, which do not affect its essential form, of the basic melodic element. Here already is established a complete unit in the work, a musical cell endowed with its own life-force and evolving about itself; and its rare quality of settled tonality, creating an impression of radiant conviction, is left unharmed by passing modulations.

The melodic phrase which forms the second

subject appears, like the first theme, in the key of E major, underlining the ground principle of unity and kinship of ideas on which the thematic disposition of the Prelude is based. We have observed on other occasions, in the *Variations symphoniques* and the *Prélude, Choral et Fugue*, that Franck as a rule never fails to observe the principle of contrasted effects prolific in musical results; but here he deliberately passes it by, in order better to create an atmosphere in which all feeling of conflict is to be excluded.

The expressive development of this second idea works gradually towards the tonality of C sharp major, preparing by a striking enharmonic change the return of the first subject, reappearing in fragments, in C sharp minor. And this momentary change of the original key, which ordinarily would darken and relax the mood of the theme to which it was applied, not only leaves the warm vigour of its rhythmic impulse untouched, but even seems to heighten the effect of cheerful energy, by some phenomenon whose actual cause would be very hard to discover. For several bars the pace and feeling quicken, drawing the melodic phrase to its culminating point, where a quick and almost dramatic interruption by a chord of the dominant seventh confirms the new key just introduced for the first time. The following grave episode has for its tonal base this same C sharp minor, relative tonality to the principal key; and in this passage the tortured theme of the Finale gradually takes shape, beneath a contrapuntal figure accompanying the contemplative main theme.

Then the main theme is restated as at the beginning in its entirety, linked on to the episode by a series of slow modulations in which the second theme of the Prelude crops up in fragments; the key is at first G flat major and then the original E major. A furtive incursion to F major sheds an instant of celestial radiance and rare sweetness, followed by a final return to the principal key; and the piece ends as it began, in a mood of contemplative, confident fervour, without any change of rhythmic beat or any unexpected move to stir its atmosphere of disciplined, invincible faith.

In itself, as an isolated composition, the fine Aria defies any comment but one founded on the most profoundly tender veneration; but considered in relation to the whole work, and for the reasons I have explained, it brings upon itself the reproach of being too little diversified. If I understand Franck's purpose, the Aria, set close to the two sections which frame it, bears the same relation to them as the central picture of a triptych to the sides. It is luminous with the bright hope which inspires the fervour of the Prelude, assuages the anguish of the Finale. The ecstatic voices of the epilogue sing its apotheosis. It is in a sense the *raison d'être* of the philosophical unity of the work, the keystone of the abstract arch which rises before our eyes. This is obvious at once from reading and study, but less easily noticed on hearing, however genuine and serious the spirit of the performance.

The listener's interest is not necessarily centred in this essential core of the composition; it fastens quite as much on what goes before and what follows. The similarity of rhythms and the use of almost identical note-values in the melodic design of the first two sections of the piece are undoubtedly responsible for this dispersed interest, but they are by no means the only cause. Between the Prelude and the Aria is a tonal kinship felt in the presence of many enharmonic points of contact, and this materially weakens the expressive value of the second section; and on paper, a similarity of the style of writing, as much in harmonic texture as in actual disposition for the piano, also adds to the impression of uniformity.

Once more, I do not attempt to condemn. I am well aware of Beckmesser and his rivals, and agree with Debussy that rules are made by works of art and not for them. I am only trying for my own interest to disentangle reasons for my opinion, and am drawn to the conclusion that in an art like music, which is only expressed in rhythm, monotony, even a sublime monotony, cannot be held a merit.

The Aria from a constructional point of view is subdivided into three sections: an introduction modulating from the Prelude to the Aria and revealing the two subjects of the piece in embryo form; the Aria proper, in song form with polyphonic variations whose agogic intensity, to use M. d'Indy's word, gradually increases; and the coda, where the first of the two themes given in the introduction reappears in a different, expanded guise. In the cyclic development of the Finale it is the recurrence of this theme from the coda which strikes the most characteristic note, since the Aria motif is only tentatively insinuated between two expositions of a feverish rhythmic figure which at last brings in an element of movement to the piece—an element until this point wholly absent. I shall not make a detailed analysis of the Aria. Words suffice for the study of musical craftsmanship, and are appropriate to the examination of an idiom or a style. They can, if absolutely necessary, describe a method of expression, and—in the composition which is now engrossing us—suggest the curving grace of the phrase which seems to bestow a benediction of transcendent melody on the slow prostrated chords of the opening, on the devout responses of the bass. Words can attempt to communicate the divine purity of the grouped quavers which twice hover over the tranquil ecstasy of a pedal A flat like a flutter of bright wings, bringing the calm radiance of the theme of the coda. They can express the swelling splendour of the rhythmic accompaniment which at every fresh statement of the principal theme grows richer and more vivid, entwining itself around it like the living vine of the Scriptures. But only the music itself, awakening here an inexpressible emotion, can exhale the precious mystic perfume, the inapprehensible, divine fragrance of communion which the coda conveys in a dozen bars instinct with love and understanding.

It is nothing short of a miracle to have made possible to a bravura instrument like the piano the privilege of expressing such static tranquil faith, to have imparted to it this rapt, ecstatic song, to have given to the astonished hands of the virtuoso the ineffable gesture of prayer.

The gusty vigour of the Finale comes straight on the heels of this revelation of spiritual ecstasy, unrolling sonorously in the bass of the instrument; Franck intended it to bring into the work a dramatic relief sufficient to renew its emotional force.

Certainly, the uneasy chromaticism of the opening argument bears out this intention; its successive expositions correspond to the refrain in the classic form of the rondo, and vary themselves by diverse modulations which make them more and more urgent, agonized, almost imperious. But the fundamental tonality, C sharp minor, binds this section with the preceding by powerful links which the listener cannot help finding a constraint; Franck should rather have separated it, abruptly broken away from the ethereal realm of contemplation and tranquillity, and hurled it with the listener into the dark torrent of human anguish or amid the agonized cries of purgatory. It is an error of judgement, which I have already noted in the linking of the Prelude and the Aria, reappearing here and bringing in its train the same weaknesses for similar reasons—kinship of rhythms and keys, made still more marked by the pieces that have gone before, and an essential similarity of pianistic method and style, in spite of the intended difference of character. The result is that just where Franck obviously counted on the relief of an antithesis, the contrast of a startling effect, he only succeeds in giving us an impression of smooth progress and continuity.

In obedience to the cyclic form on which the piece is founded, the Finale uses only a combination of themes already expressed or suggested in the course of the earlier sections. I pointed out the appearance in the Prelude of the tortured motif which first anticipates it; and this theme is developed here in four successive repetitions, each of eight bars, at first in unison in an animated rhythm of alternating semi-quavers, then hemmed in by an insistent upper dominant pedal, and finally completed, on the last two occasions, by the addition of an harmonic design in accompaniment, differentiated from a similar passage in the *Djinns* by its disposition for the instrument. Follows an episode in detached octaves with a melody of descending thirds, easily traced back to a passing phrase in the Prelude which itself seems only like a reflection of the Aria theme. In this episode we also meet the irruption of the secondary theme, stated entire several bars later under glittering trappings of triplet scales, introducing an unexpected note of chiming, ecclesiastical liveliness into the Finale. This theme, or at least the 'cell' of the theme, to use the terminology of the Schola, is also to be found in the Aria, either as constituting the motif of the introduction—which outlines the coda theme—or as giving rise to the quaver figure which, paraphrasing the introduction, separates the two elements of the principal melody one from the other.

There follows a return to the unrest and vagueness of the opening, but this time with a hint of fear amid an agitated murmur which never rises above the mezzo-forte mark even at its height. The theme of the Aria makes its appearance in the atmosphere of suspense and sombre mystery created by this dilution of tone, like a gleam of hope in the uncertainty of spiritual shadow.

A fine chromatic progression founded on a return to the opening theme leads to its re-exposition in block harmony, an outburst of grief and anguish made more intense still by the gloomy tonality of E minor.

It is followed by a slightly truncated repetition of the secondary episode, whose development leads back to a return of the theme from the Prelude, stated here in the victorious accents of a chorale, with a powerful hammered accent in the bass to maintain the rhythm of triumphal glory. Sliding by degrees from the full fervour of this earthly exaltation into a sort of mystic calm, it joins the celestial voice already heard in the coda of the Aria, an inner, pitying voice, divine Word to console and reassure. And it closes in the glorious peace of the conclusion, the slow fading of tone, the transfiguration of the theme which vanishes to nothing on the threshold of revelation, in the last hosanna of an angel chorus.

The *Prélude, Aria et Finale* was composed in the years 1886 and 1887, and heard for the first time at the Société Nationale de Musique on 12 May 1898, played by Mme Bordes-Pène, to whom the work is dedicated, a great admirer of Franck and a zealous propagandist of his instrumental music. M. Boutarel, in the *Ménestrel* of 20 May, gives a laconic but unequivocal report of it as merely 'a piece by M. Franck, long and tedious'. In the *Monde artiste* of the same date, M. Julien Torchet expressed himself at greater length but no less clearly: 'Mme Bordes-Pène played a Prelude of César Franck, a new, if not a novel, composition by this master whom I prefer to respect rather than listen to. I recommend M. César Franck to the notice of M. Camille Bellaigue, who has recently promised us a list of musicians who are boring though still living.'[1] May God grant that somebody will one day seize on the idea of devoting a line or two also to musical critics who are incompetent though dead.

I shall probably be reproached for having attempted a literary interpretation of music that is apparently only concerned with the expression of tone architecture, and which applies in the mere logic of its form a sufficiently beautiful principle to make extra-musical comment unnecessary.

Franck himself took on the responsibility for answering this criticism when he observed that the form was in his opinion only the physical body of the essential work of art, that the idea alone was the essence of the music. What is there to be said but that it is the part of the interpreter to recreate the

[1] Here is the quotation from M. Camille Bellaigue's article alluded to. It cannot be read without astonishment: 'We are feverishly busy to-day with an industrious, pompous, and boring kind of art. Boredom in music! What a fine subject for an article in our age, and what a long article! It would have to include the composer of the *Chasseur maudit*, the *Variations symphoniques* for piano and orchestra, *Ruth*, the *Béatitudes*, the man whom his zealous disciples call the French Bach, the *Master*, and who is really no more than a competent professor.'

nature and quality of this generative idea, and having identified it, or at least believing he has done it, to follow its course and emotional metamorphoses in the musical composition it begets? It may be, for the sake of argument, that he thus imposes a definite mood and precise feelings upon the thought which he is temporarily responsible for expressing, without the consent of the composer. But if we admit that the art of the performer lies at its best in the recreating of that thought, and breathing into it as natural a vitality, and as eloquent an expression, as originally inspired it, it implies that he comes to the interpretation of the finished work in the same mental state as the composer's when he was working on it.

The question is a broad one. Diderot—turning to the art of the drama—did not succeed in settling it with the *Paradoxe sur le Comédien*, and my intention now is only to set up a counter-attack to the notions of Hanslick and the theorists who, following him, refuse to allow music or its interpreters the privilege of expressing subjective emotion, limiting the former to the play of tone and rhythm and the latter to the sole duty of a technically irreproachable performance.

Some day I shall come back to this subject, for I know of none more engrossing for an interpreter who feels he has a duty at stake. For the moment, as we are concerned only with Franck's work and style, it will be enough to look for opinions in support of my contention in the literature which he knew intimately and whose doctrines he approved.

First among such works is Grétry's *Essais sur la musique*; in the fourth book he gives a whole discourse on emotions and abstract qualities and their relation to music, in the form of advice to young musicians and as the preliminary step to a method of composition. And he is not only concerned with those great stirrings of the spirit, love, sorrow, joy, ecstasy, which one expects to find underlying real inspiration; he deals in the most ingenious way with qualities of character—the liar, the flatterer, the idler, the hypochondriac, and even the man of few words, a most unexpected line for the question to take.

Further on, in the sixth book, devoted to technique, we find the following quite unambiguous remark: 'A good musical composition always involves a sentiment or an emotion, which must be expressed in its own special way.' And again: 'If a musician does not hear what a sonata means it is because the sonata does not know what it is expressing.'

It will be easy to see the possible consequences of such dicta, if one realizes the extent of Franck's admiration, in his young days, for his compatriot, the master composer of Liège, an admiration which his earlier works amply testify.

A second book, by Le Sueur, called *L'Exposé d'une musique une, imitative et particulière à chaque solennité*, is another which cannot have failed to exercise a profound influence on the style of the young organist, as it provided him with an analysis of the nature of the music required to be played during the various religious offices. And the venerable old musician, who still wielded such authority in the presbytery at the beginning of last century, makes the following remark:

'Music can imitate all the tones and inflexions of nature.

All the emotions are equally its realm, and the human heart is the living book which the composer must ever be studying.'

Several pages later, he adds, referring again to the expressive capacity of music:

'Finally, by all the use of fortes and pianos, by its different shades of meaning, by its use of quick or slow rhythm, by its notes pathetic or joyous, music can lend to an imaginary person all the emotions of which the human heart is capable; through the voice of music can be heard cries of sorrow and joy; it can convey the characters of pride and weakness, it can even express a sombre melancholy: it can communicate a religious awe, and a second after it can bring the serene emotion of hope.'

Rameau, incidentally, had already sanctioned the idea of the 'imaginary person', a far more daring conception of the interpreter's role, certainly, than the one which urges him to search for poetic impressions that the composer has not put into words. We must not overlook the fact that the writer is here concerned with the music of the church and the emotional range which was suited to it; and he would undoubtedly have authorized further imaginative licences in a musical genre less subordinated to its ends. The point is stressed in a curious essay by the Comte de Lacépède, who, not content with his work as a naturalist, undertook to write on *La Poétique de la Musique*; and here he expounds opinions whose character is amply indicated in the epigraph of Piron inscribed at the front of the book: 'Sensibility makes all our genius.' In this book we find phrases of this calibre: 'Sorrow and sweet melancholy make our true music; it is a moving picture wherein are painted all our emotions and especially our deepest emotions.' Or this: 'This is the test of your innate musicianship: are you conscious that you have received the divine gift of keen sensibility, has nature instilled into your soul imagination and feeling whose glorious song will find a response in every heart, can you touch every chord of feeling and passion, fathom every depth, and stir them effortlessly into life?'

There is a work by Villoteau which was very much in request in its day, with a title that is a programme in itself: *Recherches sur l'analogie de la musique avec les Arts qui ont pour objet l'imitation du langage*; this also contains a chapter on the point that 'it is the expression of ideas and not the combination of sounds which should be music's chief end'.

I could still go on by quoting the countless works of Jean-Jacques on the expressive qualities of music, tracing there the origins of the romantic movement which drew music into the channel of 'literary' expression, from Gluck, through Berlioz and Liszt, to Wagner, to mention only the great creative theorists. But I have said enough to establish that the work of Franck, born under these auspices and cradled in such an ideal, could not escape the strong influences which pervaded the music contemporary to his own. To hear only the technical fineness of its development without being touched by the human emotion which inspires it, to be content with formal beauty alone, would be to show oneself in utter misunderstanding of its character. Camille Saint-Saëns, himself unlikely to be accused of subordinating the logical argument of music to the musical expression of an emotion, seems to bear me out when he insists that purely musical enjoyment should be supported by a creative imagination which supplies an abstract idea to the music. He adds, 'I can see easily what art will gain by it; and I cannot see what it will lose.' A final quotation will enable me to define the duty of the ordinary conscientious pianist, face to face with the work he is anxious to interpret properly. I take it from a recent and remarkable publication by M. Pierre Lasserre, called *Philosophie du goût musical*. M. Lasserre asks himself how best to analyse the individual expressive powers of musical forms, and finds two definitions before him: the definition of the poet—the imaginative mind—describing his emotion, and the definition of the expert musician, explaining the rules of construction. And he draws the following conclusion, which is also a piece of advice:

'The two definitions are complementary and correct each other. The second prevents the first from losing itself in a vague sentimental abstraction, from emotionalizing the conditions and material technique of art; the first exalts the second by preventing it from turning everything into technical curiosities. To believe that music renews her miraculous beauty from age to age by the sole power of feeling, without any invention of tone-mechanics, is a blessed state. Only a crank could believe that she renews it by researches into acoustics, and without some noble impulse, some magnificent leap of emotion. But there are unfortunately all too many cranks among musicians to-day.'

III

The Piano Music of Gabriel Fauré

AT the moment of writing, the pianistic work of M. Gabriel Fauré is represented in the main by four series of pieces bearing titles of the type already applied to the feverishly inspired works of Frederic Chopin; and in making use of them the composer seems straight away to repudiate any literary or descriptive suggestion. These are the *Nocturnes* and the *Barcarolles*, each thirteen in number, the six *Impromptus*, and the four *Valses-Caprices*.

The list is completed by the *Thème et Variations*, the *Ballade*, originally written for solo piano and subsequently adapted as a duet for piano and small orchestra, the three *Romances sans paroles*, the *Fantaisie*, a *Mazurka*, and *Dolly*, which confides the tender secret of its baby charm to a piano duet; and here we have the entire compass of one of the most perfect pianistic productions that French music can boast.

This mere list of titles at once suggests the deferential, refined sense of tradition, and the fine temperance which with M. Fauré is uniquely blended with the most individual and sometimes the most daring independence. Certainly nothing could be more inappropriate to the fresh spontaneity of this music, with its unfailing expressive originality, than to try and adjust the spring of its emotional power to a standardized system or theory.

But I am confident that I shall take nothing from

the composer's genius if I attribute the secret of that rare harmony *de fantaisie et de raison* that he has extolled in one of his loveliest songs—that incomparable poise which has been so often and justly admired—as much to his culture as to his inspiration. It will perhaps help to an understanding of the music I propose to discuss if I quote a paragraph in which M. Fauré explains himself on this point.

In the preface to a foreign edition of the classics he makes this remark, with all the appearance of a confession of faith:

'In whatever realm of thought one takes—literature, science, art—an education which is not based on the study of the classics can be neither complete nor fundamental. . . . In the wide reaches of the human spirit, all those who have seemed to create ideas and styles hitherto unknown have only been expressing, through the medium of their own individualities, what others have already thought and said before them.'

And in another place, in the introduction to a book by M. Jean-Aubry on *French Music of To-day*, while he breaks out against certain petty nationalist tendencies which try to limit the scope and style of our contemporary art to the inspiration which evoked the ethereal delicacy of the old masters of the clavichord, and upholds the value of foreign influences which broaden our horizon, at the same time he declares himself incapable of understanding 'how school discipline can cramp expressive power, how it can get in the way of free inspiration, or why it cannot itself be made to yield emotion'.

The music born of such beliefs, as its composer clearly shows, is unlikely to bring us those crude licences, those arrogant, superficial, novelties which certain writers consider the necessary sop to originality, or even an evidence of the genuine thing.

This dignified acceptance of harmonic rule, this self-imposed discipline, is far from weakening an art which can be original without denying the past, independent without pushing tradition aside; it seems, on the contrary, to give M. Fauré's thought an added richness and a singular piquancy.

It is that his musical imagination has no need to flog itself into activity with any novelty of form or with the help of an evocative or suggestive argument, in order to reveal its creative force and awaken in us the echo of feelings hitherto unexpressed.

It carries with it an expressive value which enables him to dispense with the assistance of the striking or the picturesque effect. It regulates the idiom of a style disciplined to follow the delicate course of a new thought. It evolves freely amid rules whose order and logic are thus supported and rejuvenated. And neither learning nor culture has left on M. Fauré the deplorable imprint alleged so violently by the enemies of the classics and by those who despise academicism.

They only made it easier for him to recognize the guiding principles, persisting under the changing face of beauty through the ages, that would help the harmonious flowering of his tender genius and insight. And, using a language which has never tried to astonish or to compel attention, he has set on his masterpieces the hallmark of a surprising and permanent freshness.

M. Fauré's piano compositions are not among the earliest in the list of his published work. The three *Romances sans paroles* which stand at the beginning of the series of pieces to be discussed in this essay are numbered Op. 17, and were not published till 1880.

But in the accompaniments of the vocal works written before then, and similarly in the piano part of the Op. 13 sonata or of the Op. 15 quartet, those peculiarities of style can already be detected which to this day have remained the outward and visible signs of his art, and make it so strongly individual.

There is not a trace here, it is true, of what the mere lay-out of a work by Liszt, or Chopin, or Debussy, or Albeniz, is enough to disclose—a fundamental regeneration of pianistic technique. Here, as in all M. Fauré's work, the true novelty lies in the quality of the musical texture much more than in an unusual style of writing.

This does not imply that he does not make use of technical ingenuity and a variety of striking methods in pieces of rapid rhythm or lively character. I need only cite as examples the Scherzo of the first violin and piano sonata, or the *Impromptus*, or the sprightly episodes in the *Valses-Caprices*, all of which combine play of tone and rhythm with grace and inventive charm.

But in my opinion M. Fauré's real pianistic originality is revealed in the works of a contemplative or softly impassioned nature, where an intimate emo-

tion inspires a style that is deeply intense and controlled at the same time, expressed in a pianistic
language which seems to exhale a secret warmth. It
is to be felt in the emotional mood of the *Nocturnes*,
where the night's dreamy ecstasy matches a rapturous
or melancholy song; or in the exotic languor of the
Barcarolles, where the soft splash of water mingles
with the happy murmur of love; or in the grave
serenity which breathes through many of the
Préludes, and the splendid *Variations*.

And if the choice of mood, the very reticence of
the titles selected, seem that they must inevitably
dull the brilliance or limit the tone colour which
translates them into music, at least they invest it with
a quality which belongs to no other music that has
ever been written.

He has a habit of frequently writing broken chords
to replace simultaneous harmonies, but there is a
diversity in the method which constantly renews the
interest of an idiom in itself a little monotonous.
The linked chords thus written, often shared between
the two hands, take on a plastic, astonishing, suppleness which seems to arrest the curve of melody
emerging from them in mid air, and to form a
gossamer veil of sound about it.

Again, there is intense, expressive point in those
sustained phrases, such as might occur in a string
quartet, full of throbbing modulations, whose
separate voices hover outside the tonality which
secretly holds them like glowing, tremulous trails
of tone, suddenly reblended and released by an
unexpected and yet inexorable harmonic turn.

There is a peculiarly happy choice of rhythms; sometimes their even poise ensures the rhythmic sweep of a musical phrase, whose harmonious inflexions will now and then follow the metre of verse, with its deferred endings and even its rhyme; or sometimes by their syncopations and cross-rhythms, and the characteristic suspensions or retardations of the bass, they accentuate the agitated intensity of a development or of a progression; there is a meticulous care for the balance of tone, a puristic abhorrence of the doubling of notes that coarsens and thickens it, and perfect discretion in use of extreme registers.

Finally, there is his inimitable note of poetry in an entirely personal pianistic style, where everything renovates itself without any perceptible change, where the ornamentation is embodied in the melody that it enfolds or extends, and where, even though usually it was conceived and written at his desk, there is as much grace and spontaneity as in the brilliant virtuoso music that springs to life under the fingers.

In the ensuing analysis I have chosen to follow the chronological order of publication rather than to group the pieces by their type, which would undoubtedly be more rational and exact; and this with the desire to follow out, work by work, the expressive course of a musical inspiration which has mirrored, with a fidelity unmatched in any other French composer, the emotional curve of feelings modified as the years have gone by.

The music of Gabriel Fauré bears, therefore, an

almost autobiographical sincerity which imprints an indefinable quality of human tenderness on the smallest of his works; and it reveals the throbbing of a profound and constant sensitiveness beneath the perfectly draped veil of the work of art and the patrician exterior at which the admirer in a hurry to judge and classify all too often stops short.

The explanation of M. Fauré's work, up to about Op. 38—that is, if we are to accept this summary classification of the emotions which pierce deep and intermingle through the cool impersonality of his titles—lies in the fleeting, sensuous delight of living day by day, the seductive richness of dreams, the emotions and longings of youth. Later, up to the ninth *Nocturne*, it lies in the emotional glow of maturity, the conscious, passionate conflict of feeling. And lastly, from the time of *Penelope* and including it, it lies in a transcendent quality of grave sustained beauty and fervour to which a refining and etherealizing musical style communicates a sort of moral serenity.

In the pages that follow I shall try to describe these expressive modifications, but I earnestly beg the reader to compare the musical text side by side with the commentary; this essay has no other end than to emphasize beauties whose caressing quality and inherent poetry can never be translated into words.

While hinting at the youthful personality of their composer, the three *Romances sans paroles* are already charged with the full perfume of his mature works; they were not published, as I have observed, until 1880, when M. Fauré was thirty-five.

French Piano Music

The first has all the melancholy grace of an expressive colloquy; the inner part lovingly twines itself round the melodic fluctuations of the upper part and accompanies it, note by note, in tender, clinging accents. The second, unconsciously Mendelssohnian in cast, breaks out with an unruly, charming ardour enhanced by the flying rush of the accompaniment. And in the soft, resigned mood of the third the imitation which discreetly extends the original melody weaves itself in with infinite charm, and the figure whose sweet inflexion adorns the last two measures bears an infinite purity.

They are only sketches: but short and slight as they are, they stand out in the facile genre to which they belong on account of their natural lyrical perfection; and under a surface which suggests improvisation there can already be discerned the careful pains for the finished form and for the felicitous detail which was to mark Fauré's later compositions with so personal a style.

The *Ballade*, Op. 19, was more fortunate from the point of view of publication than the *Romances sans paroles*; it also appeared in 1880, as soon as it was completed, in its original form for piano solo. M. Fauré's individuality manifests itself from the first in the entirely novel conception of a form which romanticism seemed to have destined to the exclusive expression of passionate and heady emotion. This work, on the contrary, is lapped in a calm atmosphere of controlled emotion and quiet happiness, emphasizing an instrumental technique that is deliberately light and pellucid. Joseph de Marliave, in his re-

Gabriel Fauré

markable *Études Musicales*, tells us that it was written after an impression of the forest scene in *Siegfried*.

A dreamy exposition, with a theme which is to be used as the second subject in the softly animated section which follows it; a bridge passage, whose pastoral note is itself derived from part of the twentieth bar of the opening andante, and is the germ both of the joyous vigour of the middle allegro, and the ecstatic murmur of the last section; and three lively episodes, bound together by the sentiment of tender exaltation born of the short descending melodic phrase which is common to them all and which takes on their respective rhythms : these are the elements of this work, shimmering exquisitely with sunshine and light, turning the gentle melancholy of the night into the wonder of a spring morning. They are rather modulations in one prevailing lyrical mood than variations in the academic sense; but they are united and controlled by a hidden logic, and their rhapsodic nature is balanced by a scrupulous care for unity and proportion.

The grace of the orchestral version, where the added instruments relieve the piano score of part of its harmonic framework, seems to me greater still than that of the edition for solo piano. The variety of timbres accentuates, yet without allowing it to predominate, the play of a translucent, quicksilver virtuosity, the swirl of arpeggios, the rushing flight of scales, the mad ripple of trills, and from this point of view holds several attractive modifications.

The first *Impromptu*, Op. 25, has the lay-out and

rhythmic plan of a quick barcarolle. Its ripple of
singing water is like a barcarolle, and accompanied
in the same way by a light-hearted and yet unremit-
ting harmonic oscillation; and in the inner part,
above the swing of relaxed rhythm, that warm
passionate song which soothes the evening's melancholy is the very voice echoed in the first *Barcarolle*
in A minor which follows it—Op. 26, written in
1882. This lyric piece glides over noiseless, silver
waters in the quiet wake of arpeggios. A hint of
suspended minor tonality lends it a languid, half-
smiling, half-melancholy charm; one does not know
whether it veils a regret or a hint of coquetry.

With the first *Valse-Caprice*, Op. 30, written in
1883, M. Fauré modernizes and restores to a fine
proportion the out-moded form beloved of the
Restoration salons and racked by the plaintive
lyricism of Chopin. In M. Fauré's hands the genre
becomes at once caressing and whimsical, alive with
the play of tone and rhythm, in which furtive gusts
of passion and murmured vows, the more significant
for being only whispered, pass and repass. Before he
wrote the four pieces which form the series of the
Valses-Caprices, and are among the most individual
works he ever composed, one would never have
suspected that music so glib and sparkling, whose
worldly nature is never glossed over, could have
retained so much sensuous charm, distinction, and
impassioned tenderness.

One would imagine that the nimble fantasy of
these pieces could hardly bear the constraint of a
fixed form; yet it is the considered harmoniousness

of their themes and the logic of their development, more even than the self-styled caprice, that engenders their power to charm. Their contours are moulded to a hidden line, like the frame-foundation which maintains the exquisite, fragile pose of little wax figures.

The first *Valse* is a perfect pattern of form, homogeneous, fine, and delicate. The first theme has a delicious virginal freshness as it glides among a deft rush of arpeggios falling around it with the soft rustle of silk; in response comes the lavish briskness of a strongly marked rhythm, fined slowly down by a gossamer thread of embroidery woven around it which brings back the grace of the opening tempo. Then, above an undercurrent of beating quavers maintaining the rhythm of the dance, a middle section is interposed in the form of an infinitely tender dialogue. The second theme is repeated, and impelled towards the conclusion by a brilliant peroration, when after the conventional dominant seventh chord which seems to hover in suspense over the last note, a dreamy, languorous coda opens like the memory of a moment of happiness recalled, and moves with gradually quickening pace to the conclusion.

With slight differences of mood, the later *Valses-Caprices* show a similar construction.

The second *Impromptu*, Op. 31, in F minor, which appeared the same year, has an animated tarantella movement, divided into halves by the expressive interposition of a major section which sets a relaxed triple measure and softly exotic harmonies against a rhythmic insistence in the bass. It is, actually, the scheme of the first *Impromptu*— but a little more individualized and nearer to the perfect model of the third.

I can pass over the Op. 32 *Mazurka*, which, although also published in 1883, bears only a distant relation to the rest of the remarkable works of this period; it is probably of all M. Fauré's compositions the one least indicative of his individuality.

The chronological order we have followed up to this point has shown us only works of a lively, almost joyous mood, in which M. Fauré has delighted in evoking in musical tone the pleasures and emotions of youth. The year of 1883 was his most prolific period of pianistic work, for we find no less than seven published pieces; this year brings us for the first time into touch with an elegiac vein of singular lyric charm, where even the deepest expression of sentiment has no trace of sentimentality, where style keeps its aristocratic note, where passion is in the service of beauty.

The three *Nocturnes* of Op. 33 may not have the unforgettable beauty of the sixth, seventh, and ninth, where M. Fauré's piano music attains the level of the greatest of all time; but though they still belong to the inspirational phase born of serene spiritual happiness, none the less they express an everbroadening, passionate sensibility. In the mood of the first *Nocturne*, in E flat minor, the dominating note is already a sorrow-laden emotion, never before expressed in music, surely, with such nobility and truth. A slow, tortured melody, whose expressive curve descends from the unreal inflexions of the piano's highest register to the muffled and almost funereal tone of the middle of the instrument, lies over an even rhythm of softly measured chords. Then without change of key or, hardly, of pace, sweeps in the strong sea breeze of a passage whose picturesque nature is enhanced by the rolling swell of the bass.

A change to flowing rhythm leads to a melodic episode of about ten bars, full of inexpressible melancholy; its almost motionless oscillation seems to hold in it all the infinite loneliness of the sea. After a recapitulation of these latter elements in dialogue form, stirred and troubled by pathetic harmonies, the original theme reappears, accompanied this time by a slow, monotonous lapping of still waters, still further heightening the effect of melancholy. Then a twice-breathed weary sigh, heavy with intolerable distress, breaks the silence of the night; and this fine tone poem, which complements—or anticipates—the sentiment of songs like the *Berceaux* or the *Cimetière*, is at an end.

Neither the elegance nor the cultured technique of the preceding works had disclosed the individual quality of M. Fauré's pianistic inspiration as this work does. In this *Nocturne* everything is new: inspiration, tonal relations, form, and harmonic style. And it should be added that they combine to make a musical interpretation which equals in expressive perfection the beauty of the feeling that lies behind it.

The musical texture of the second *Nocturne*

seems to me to be less rich, or rather, less expressive, in spite of the similarity of the musical scheme. As in the first *Nocturne* the themes and rhythms seem to breathe the lyrical feeling of the tide slowly ebbing at night-time, and the development of melodies shares a similar quality; but the note is more nebulous, less persuasive, and the sea does not give up its secret sorrows. Yet the comparison would be unfair if it prevented us from feeling the gentle melancholy of the opening bars and the sinewy, deliberate precision of the second theme, overlaid by an expressive phrase whose melodic freedom makes a skilful contrast with the persistent thematic rhythm of the accompaniment.

The third *Nocturne*, in A flat, is fragrant with tenderness and charm. It takes us back to that happy expression of feeling which the first two *Nocturnes*, the first above all, had for the time put away, those first profound forewarnings of a new emotion whose poignant note was to be set down in the works to come.

This nocturne sings anew of the perfumed ecstasy of twilight, a lyric in which every note is heavy with the caress of love. No conflict of feeling, no clash of mood interrupts, to destroy the unity of its warm, sensuous melody, the languid peace of its harmonies and measured pace.

I have already spoken of the third *Impromptu* in A flat, also published in 1883, as the perfect pattern of these short pieces whose proportions are poised delicately on the felicitous contrast of two parent ideas. Indeed, in this piece there exists so rare a harmony between the choice of themes, their fresh and youthful sentiment, the nice balance of their alternating phrases, and the high quality of its pianistic writing, with the light tracery of the passage for the left hand, as it detaches itself from a nebulous background, that no other work of the kind, one feels, could possibly give a more lovely sensation of refined and easy perfection.

The fourth and fifth *Nocturnes*, Op. 36 and 37, both appeared in 1885. They are analogous in the expression of a single idea, once more full of erotic desire. The fifth *Nocturne*, it is true, sets against the soft question of its first theme the contrast of an agitated interlude. But its true significance is not so much in the passing gloom which burdens the first few bars as in the passionate warmth of its development.

The fourth *Nocturne* is steeped in dreamy longing, mingling with the slow chimes of evening bells, carrying the memory of regrets and rapture, languishing for the lost delights of an exiled love.

Here we have a hint of that secret labour over detail which was able to modify an emotion without altering its essence, to lend it a sort of deeper and nobler restlessness, a sustained ardour; it is to be observed twice in the 'transition' period of M. Fauré's work. Then, there breaks out all over again the fullness of a tranquil inspiration master of its medium for expression, justifying the considered choice of method and form by new works still loftier and more beautiful.

French Piano Music

And so it is with the *Valse-Caprice*, Op. 38, also dating from 1885; though the form is almost identical with that of the first *Valse*, in A major, one cannot help recognizing traces of this transition under the grace and vivacity of the themes; it is a kind of feverish melancholy which impresses one perhaps the more for seeming bound to the joyous rhythm which bears it along.

The second and third *Barcarolles*, Op. 41 and 42, appeared in 1886; here, again, is this strong note of introspection, this unsatisfied desire. The rhythm and the mood are almost the same as in the first *Barcarolle*—or the first *Impromptu* that I compared to it—but they do not seem to evoke the poetry of love and rippling water with so much liquid charm and tender insouciance. And even if the technical elegance of these two works is impeccable, and they are the product of the same search for clarity and logic which makes them musically the match of these earlier works, all the same they create an impression of distant aloofness, and almost of indifference, which is quite the last quality to be expected from the music of M. Fauré. The development impresses one as perhaps overworked for the type of theme and the evanescent quality of the emotion; the ornamentation seems to weigh it down without enriching it, and almost to impede the blossoming of a melodic phrase which recalls the curves of his earlier manner. There is a kind of inner disharmony about it; but far from deprecating it, we should cherish it with a singular affection, because it was from this uncertain period, this 'awkward age' of M. Fauré's work, that a new beauty was to flower and mature; and to this we owe the finest expression of his art.

In the course of the same year the fourth *Barcarolle*, Op. 44, revives for a moment the tender 'Fauré' enchantment of the early works. For here, again, in the perfection of a few short pages, is a lazy fantasy of rhythm which lulls to sleep a joyous, subtle melody and the exotic scent of the lagoons mingling with the languor of a passionate song.

After the fourth *Barcarolle* and for a space of nearly eight years, M. Fauré abandoned all piano composition. The interval was filled with a succession of vocal works, the stage music for *Shylock* and *Caligula*, the poignant *Requiem*, and the fine second quartet. But though he waited some time—too long, in my own selfish opinion—before once more making the solo piano the channel of a musical inspiration which ennobled and exalted it, he never ceased to embody it in most of his other work; the accompaniments to the immortal songs written at this time, with the piano part of the second quartet, witness the advance in his instrumental powers.

There is, however, to be included in this period, although it was not published till 1894, the enchanting little suite for four hands called *Dolly*, numbered Op. 56. The six short pieces which compose this lyric contain the most engagingly intimate nuances of babyhood, and are the only pieces in M. Fauré's work to which he intentionally gave other titles than those of absolute music.

French Piano Music

There are only brief indications of character or feeling: Berceuse, Mi-a-ou, Le Jardin de Dolly, Kitty-Valse, Tendresse, and Le Pas espagnol. But music more explicit than the words expresses them, shot through with the rebellious grace, the deep ingenuous dreams, the ecstatic surprise and the joy of childhood; still more, like Schumann in the *Kinderscenen* or Debussy in the *Children's Corner*, with the tender affection of the composer.

M. Fauré's return to pianistic composition was heralded by the publication in 1893 of the third *Valse-Caprice*. There is in this work a sinewy rhythm, a firm line, a command of the instrument and of form, and a kind of sensitive dignity (if these words can at all define the quality of a music which still holds to its episodic character), very significant of the importance and nature of the change, in the composer's spirit during the eight years of which I have just spoken. There is as ever the sovereign grace of a style of which every line is an enchantment to the ear and to the spirit, but the grip is surer and more mature; there is still the magic of a melodic curve whose touch is, as ever, exquisitely surprising, but there is also the tightening up of pianistic technique, revealed in brilliance and verve with as much felicity as in the previous delicacy.

I will only mention as an example the transformation of themes in the interlude, the robust passion which renders them plastic and varied, together with the expressive warmth of the developments and the ingenious play of virtuosity. It is already, in fact, the unerring, keen note of the *Bonne Chanson*, endowing the rhythms of yesterday with an unexpected vivacity and character.

The fourth *Valse-Caprice*, Op. 62, dated 1894, supplies a different turn of sentiment, but the same harmony of musical and pianistic expression. The persuasive insistence of the first rhythm lends the whole piece a wistful tenderness not to be dispelled by all the ironic vivacity of the second theme and the arch caprice of the developments which spread from it. Even an ebullient coda cannot overlay this slender, driving impulse which persists through it and throbs for the last time in the silence following the happy tumult of the peroration.

In the same year comes the sixth *Nocturne*, Op. 63, an incomparable climax of that patrician ascent which has led us upwards from the cheerful delights of a joyous music to the highest possible expression of human emotion.

There are few works in the literature of music to compare with this, and in M. Fauré's work nothing reflects better the loftiness of his musical inspiration. The emotion distilled from this piece transcends the bounds of personal feeling to attain that state of universal aspiration which is the hall-mark of the masterpiece.

From the first note of the fine exposition something in us grows warm and tender as we listen, as though this song, laden with contemplation and thought, were confiding to us the secret of a sadness never expressed before. Then, timid and hesitant, though full of latent passion, a second theme creeps in, grows bolder and finally breaks out in an out-

burst of grief which brings back the broad melody of
the opening. A silence follows, sustaining quivering
chords, and a voice is lifted above a flutter of stirring
leaves, so sweet and consoling that it illumines with
a shaft of light the rich progression built upon the
repetition of the second theme. The phrase swells to
insistence and to exhaustion, following the principle
of modulation which was to become so dear to M.
Fauré, and then as though broken with the effort it
fades away in an eddy of tone.

Again, and more poignant still because it follows
this impassioned outburst without any preparation,
the resigned and confiding melody of the opening is
heard in the compassionate darkness. And so, with
a simplicity whose sad beauty defies the power of
words to express, closes that work of M. Fauré's
which, with the *Theme and Variations*, is in my
opinion the most perfect.

The fifth *Barcarolle*, Op. 66 (1894), is to the other
Barcarolles what the sixth *Nocturne* is to the rest of
the *Nocturnes*; it dominates the others by a similar
emotional concentration, and reveals the same inner
brilliance. No longer is it the quiet vision of dreaming canals in a soft Venetian distance where a gon-
dola glides silently by and emotion is slender and
evanescent. This great wind swells the harmonies
like flying sails on the open sea. The wild, free
passion of Antony and Cleopatra is awakened by
these powerful rhythms and it is the keel of their
splendid bark that we glimpse against the distant
luminous splendour of the West.

The delightful sixth *Barcarolle*, Op. 70, written in

1896, abandons the warm ardour of the preceding work for a feeling more tranquil and more controlled. Yet the play of sunlight on this stretch of sparkling water, rippled by a morning breeze, reflects in its own individual way the gradual change of inspiration and style whose course we are following. M. Fauré's allegro style becomes more lucid, its rhythm more alive; it aims further now than the ensnaring of a passing passionate moment. And his andante style holds a note of new concentrated passion and tenderness, as it were a more virile emotional force.

This greater firmness of musical thought is reflected in a similar modification of instrumental style. The arpeggio patterns, though persisting as the basis of M. Fauré's pianistic idiom, are less glibly fluent; they are part of the music and enhance its modulations instead of softening and shading them off as before.

The web of harmony is at once freer and closer knit, and the bold rhythmic precision of chords is often called in to strengthen the themes. The artistic medium is now perfectly wedded to the inspirational idea. And a new work, the *Theme and Variations*, written in 1896, M. Fauré's most important composition both in actual dimensions and in character and beauty, sets a magnificent seal on this perfect harmony.

The theme has five phrases, alternating regularly, of contrasting timbres, and creates a seriousness like a Greek frieze where weeping maidens, drawn by the rhythm of an inexorable fate, stand in sorrowful tears. The poignant simplicity of its melody is graven on our hearts; it is sustained in each variation, not by the clever devices of craftsmanship, but by the trans-figuring of its own lyrical essence—as in the later Beethoven variations, where in each fresh change the melody persists as an emanating essence, in perfect clarity.

A chaste semiquaver counterpoint in the first variation encircles a second statement of the theme, reduced to only three sections, and in the left hand. The second variation takes the melody and divides it into fragments, impelled on by a lively ascending figure whose harmony retains the original character of the theme. The same driving vigour stamps the transformation of the fundamental theme in the third variation, where the theme leaps out, returns, and rebounds in the quick alternation of duple and triple beat; this is followed by the poetic ardour of the fourth variation, lashed into foam by a motif of spaced notes crossing over from one hand to the other, and calmed down for a second by an accent of tender entreaty. And then the lofty *élan* of the fifth, the grave tranquillity of the sixth, the poignant, exalted mood, trembling with overflowing passion, of the seventh, the mystic peace of the eighth, and the dark, lifted ecstasy of the ninth variation, where on that G sharp high on the curve of melody, the heart sinks down like a star in the evening.

After this surges the mystic flight of the tenth variation, where the feverish haste of the left hand is held back by the timidity of the right in a constraint that proves exasperating till in a fury it breaks away and finishes in a triumphant crescendo.

Gabriel Fauré

Finally the eleventh; with the fine expressive conclusion in the major bringing compassionate grace and consolation, a gathered serenity of emotion, blended by the tranquil and persuasive notes of the theme in the bass.

The wealth of material in this work, its depth of emotion, and the quality of its musical texture make it undoubtedly one of the finest and most precious things in the literature of the piano for all time. It alone is enough to defend French music of our time from the glib critic whose battery of reproaches includes those of frivolity and of desiccated elegance, to say no more.

In 1899 a new *Nocturne* was published, the seventh, Op. 74; and like the one in E flat, it has its being in the purest and loftiest realms of musical feeling. A first episode is divided into two sections which mutually respond and fuse into each other, the one contemplative and restrained, the other more animated, almost restless. Then a distant chiming of bells; a mere trembling in the air, and then the soft caress of a melody instinct with youthful emotion. Gradually it rises to a feverish height, loses itself in a dream, exhausting a new mood of blossoming ecstasy in a warm return of the first theme. And then peace again in the sweet nocturnal stirring of breeze on innocent slumbers.

A fresh period of silence which lasted four years came to an end in 1903 by the appearance of the eight *Pièces brèves*; these have been christened in later editions, by the whim of a publisher anxious no doubt to increase his sales, with seductive titles not anticipated by the composer.

Consequently the first piece is dubbed a ' Capriccio', the second—a sort of slender *Romance sans paroles*—'Fantaisie', and the *Andante molto moderato* of the fourth labelled 'Adagietto'. The fifth is called 'Improvisation' and matches the title well in its free natural vivacity. The seventh, close kin to *Nell*, bears the title—how unlike Fauré—of 'Allégresse'. And the short eighth piece is elevated to the rank of the eighth *Nocturne*.

The third and sixth alone have retained their real identity—of fugue. But we can assume that they were only abandoned to their fate with a sigh. As a whole these *Pièces brèves*, whose general title is excellently adequate, have a very attractive charm and the *Fugues* especially are finely conceived and carried out.

The seventh *Barcarolle* is Op. 90, and the fourth *Impromptu* Op. 91; both appeared in 1906, published by Heugel; after having enriched the catalogues of his first publisher Hamelle with nearly a hundred masterpieces, and certainly without any great profit to himself, M. Fauré decided to establish relations with this other firm, and did so until 1913, when he transferred the publication of his works to Durand.

The *Impromptu* discloses a wild rejuvenescence. Here is the whimsical freshness and joyous vigour of his first compositions, with a more poignant feeling in the middle section, where the mark of ripe maturity reappears. The skilful and charming development of this piece is built on a contrapuntal idiom so natural that its ornamentation seems no more than the lovely flower of a fresh inspiration. Here is one of the many inimitable traits of M. Fauré's music—this transformation of the dustiest academic rules of composition into novel, glowing detail and emotional phrase.

Under a deliberately austere aspect, the seventh *Barcarolle* expresses a grim, uneasy voluptuousness, lit by luminous, caressing moments, where harmonies melt into a light shiver of diatonic quavers. There are unmistakable signs here of this second phase of evolution, in which M. Fauré's inspiration was slowly to dissociate itself from a musical idiom too loaded with external graces for the emotion he wished to express. The gay, decided rhythm of the eighth *Barcarolle* (which followed in 1908) creates a momentary illusion of the irrepressible nonchalance of yesterday, but the austerity of the development, the bold clarity of the modulations, and the moving, melancholy pathos of the second theme turn us inevitably towards the new lyricism of spirit which the ninth *Nocturne* presents in its almost final form—Op. 97, written also in 1908.

Here, within the sheath of a pianistic style of apparently the simplest kind, throbs the driving hidden eloquence of a harmonic speech which seems to grow in intensity in proportion as it is liberated from extraneous decoration. What wealth of expressive power lies in that phrase which irresistibly, as though in an agony of tenderness, evokes the fine lyrical passage in B major which closes the piece.

French Piano Music

The dedication of this work makes it more valuable in my eyes and doubly dear; but setting aside this personal feeling, it still seems to me that there is here revealed for the first time, at least in so perfect a harmony of mood and technique, the passionate and yet contemplative quality of a musical emotion whose secret only M. Fauré could unfold to us.

Op. 99, the tenth *Nocturne*, written in 1909, is of analogous inspiration and plan. Like the foregoing work, it is constructed upon a slow and poignant rising phrase which works into a fine sonorous major. It revels for a moment in this sanguine mood and then falls back into the melancholy of the opening key.

In the ninth *Barcarolle*, Op. 100 (1909), there is a wistful echo, as it were, of happiness long past. It exhales a sweet perfume of vanished days; and the deft vivacity of a piano style more superficial than in the two *Nocturnes* I have just discussed seems to be painting in the dying contours of lovely, distant shadows.

The fifth *Impromptu*, Op. 102, dates from the same year, and is a fantasy of persistent, recurrent design. It is formed on a diatonic figure in whole tones which turns and whirrs ceaselessly under pressure of an ostinato figure in minims. The resulting impression is of a sort of pulsating hallucination, rare in M. Fauré's work. The scherzos of the second quartet and third quintet are other possible instances.

A series of *Préludes* follow, the first three published in 1910, and the last six in 1911, forming as

Gabriel Fauré

Op. 103 certainly one of M. Fauré's most distinctive works. They compel attention by their emotional power, harmonic richness, grave seriousness and strength of feeling, as much as by the versatile pianistic technique which, effortlessly renewing its capacity, imprints upon each one a unique tone quality without impairing the remarkable unity of the whole series.

The sixth *Impromptu* is Op. 86, but was not published till 1913, and is actually only a transcription for the piano of a piece originally written and published for the harp. The rare beauty of the themes remains, but the ingenuity of their transcription does not in my opinion succeed in creating in the new version the specialized tonal charm of the instrument which inspired the work. The title only vaguely suggests the character of this piece, which is actually more like a fantasy or a ballade.

The piano pieces become rarer, since M. Fauré was at this time absorbed in the composition of *Pénélope*; in this gloriously noble dramatic poem, coloured with inexpressible tenderness and fervour, he reaffirms the powerful mastery of a musical thought which was never loftier nor more passionate, nor more amazingly and directly individual than in this.

Yet by good fortune there are several works contemporary with this masterpiece which mirror its spirit and its tendencies on the piano. In the first place, a moving elegy—the eleventh *Nocturne*, Op. 104, No. 1, written in 1913—dedicated to the memory

of Noémi Lalo. There is no more touching lament
written than this work, grave and charged with emotion; its chaste outlines and controlled passion have
the reticence and mournful dignity of an antique
tomb.

In delightful contrast with this *Nocturne* is the
tenth *Barcarolle*, Op. 104, No. 2, published in the
same year. In this sketch, misty with clouded hues,
you will find neither the sensuous ecstasy nor the
exotic grace of the earlier works in the genre. Only
the melancholy of one tone, grey upon grey, which
is sufficient to create the most ethereal and delicate of
atmospheres. The music drifts on a stirring breeze
of melody like a slow sail under a hazy sky.

The eleventh *Barcarolle*, Op. 105, which appeared
in 1914, presents an unexpected conclusion in a
major key, which is not without a philosophical
significance, too, and at the same time a number of
pianistic novelties which stimulate the interest of a
rhythm which is, it must be admitted, less original
than that of the preceding work.

Both the twelfth *Barcarolle*, Op. 106, and the
twelfth *Nocturne*, Op. 107, appeared in 1916. The
Barcarolle is charming and joyous, softly glowing,
and its rhythmic balance evokes none of the sad
mystery of its predecessors. The *Nocturne*, on the
contrary, is agonized and poignant, a wanderer in a
waste of desolate misery. It takes an unusual form,
opening with a long phrase twice repeated, passing
straight into a sort of troubled peroration which
is actually the first phrase repeated at twice its pace;
and this arresting melodic metamorphosis creates

the striking effect of an outburst of grief that knows no bounds.

In concluding the study of an incomparable artistic output, which these pages, in the effort to express the inner lyricism that breathes so vital a life into it, will only have very briefly and coldly outlined, I have only to mention the *Fantaisie* for piano and orchestra, Op. 111, written in 1919.

It may be that the very musical quality of this work, the reserved dignity of the themes, the nobility of its balance, and the restraint of feeling which it expresses, are not perfectly attuned to the conventional treatment of a dialogue between the piano and the orchestra. Those who love contrast and colour will no doubt deplore the restraint with which the orchestra is treated, confined as it is with anxious care for tonal balance within the limits of accompaniment; and on the other hand they will complain that the piano part is not written in the brilliant style, rich with superficial graces, full of solid harmonies, and drowned in pedalling, which allows the solo instrument to hold its own against the overwhelming nearness of orchestral tone and the proportions of a concert-room.

These criticisms—or these reserves—would, in my estimation, only be justified if M. Fauré had intended to write a Concerto and had set aside the customary and often formidable technical apparatus which is part of it. But here, on the contrary, it is surely possible to appreciate the perfect mating of technical method to the nature of the inspiration and to the lyrical character of the work. Simply and quietly, without any pretentious preparation, the piano states a lucid, concise melody, and the orchestra repeats it. A soft dialogue follows, surrounded by slender arabesques of arpeggios, enlivened now and then by a flash of animation. A moment's silence; then on an insistent beat whose last bars already suggest a rising impatience, a rich melody in triple time is outlined, striking a vivid contrast, in its warm eloquence, with the elegant immobility of the opening. The first episode now reappears, superficially almost the same as in its original exposition, though perhaps a shade more arrogant and assured, as though galvanized into life by the thrilling atmosphere of the intervening passage; and a well-knit development draws it on to a brilliant conclusion.

In the scheme of this composition everything comes within the range of a chamber music in which there are merely more instruments used than usual. Thus there was every reason for the exclusion of the highly coloured or the virtuoso effect in a work in which M. Fauré consciously avoided such facile charm. Let us congratulate him on having bestowed upon this composition—in which I am honoured in the dedication and of which I was the first interpreter—a concentrated emotion and a lofty exaltation of feeling which cannot fail to draw the attention not only of pianists but of musicians generally.

And so for the time being closes the list of pianistic works of the greatest French composer of our time. The study I have undertaken will not have proved useless if it has stimulated a fresh reading of the musical texts which have inspired it, to savour once

Gabriel Fauré

more their inexpressible quality, their intense sweet poetry, and their inimitable originality.[1]

[1] I remind readers that this article was published in Fauré's life-time, in 1922. I added then a postscript: 'I regret to be unable to do anything but mention here the publication, almost at the same time as this, of a new, very fine *Barcarolle*, the thirteenth, Op. 116, and of an expressive *Nocturne*, Op. 119, also the thirteenth of the series.'

I did not think that these works would be, alas, the last to be written for the instrument he loved above all, by the master and friend for whose loss we are still inconsolable. It will be found, on reading them, that they contain all the qualities of sad enchantment which mark the works of the last period. Few notes, but each one fraught with meaning. The least possible of technical working out is here once more linked, almost paradoxically, with an intensity of musical emotion. The interest of the posthumous publication, through the exertions of the publisher Schneider, of two cadenzas for the Concertos by Beethoven, and Mozart, both in C minor, is oddly heightened by the fact that, in these improvisations, one of which dates from 1869, and the other from 1902, we find peculiarities of style and technique of a striking resemblance, and inspired by the purest classicism.

IV

The Piano Music of Emmanuel Chabrier

IT is at one and the same time concise and exuberant, spontaneous and refined. The genial, high-flavoured, free and easy gaiety that fills it seems in no way to impair its emotional delicacy. It achieves the paradox of often expressing musical ideas that are deliberately naïve in language of overflowing sensuousness; of effecting a surprising mixture of middle-class high spirits and Bacchic frenzy.

Above all, Chabrier's piano music throbs with a constantly insistent beating rhythm, whose regular pulse is perceptible even in moments of the most languorous tenderness. And yet there hardly exists a musical style that creates better than this the suggestion of untrammelled fancy, or that seems nearer to free improvisation. To those who know the concentrated labour and painstaking care that Chabrier gave to his smallest compositions, this discloses a contradiction that gives his indomitable gaiety a far greater, almost an emotional value. For none of that patient revision, nor those carefully weighed up retouches, were able to stifle the ebullience of first inspiration. To my mind this is the real clue to the performance of Chabrier's work, to understand how to keep intact that irrepressible spontaneity, that leaping vitality, which are there revealed triumphant over a sometimes inadequate power of expression, and to make manifest the victory of natural genius over a tardy technique.

Emmanuel Chabrier

In the following pages it is my intention to try to define the spirit and to analyse the method of an artist in whom is to be found the clear-cut originality of personality as well as the strong natural evidences of race and tradition. And to show that his work was so full of significance for the future of French music that its repercussion is not even exhausted to-day.

We cannot conceive of Debussy, Paul Dukas, Florent Schmitt, Ravel, and Gustave Charpentier, not even of Erik Satie—at least not as the men we know them to be—without being reminded of the existence of Chabrier at the most significant moment of the formidable outbreak of Wagnerism in France. The importance of this assumption is certainly well above the intrinsic value of the work I am proposing to study. But, viewing it from this angle, we are better able to realize the value of the role played in the history of our art by this stocky, corpulent, waggish Auvergnat, given to extremes of excitement as of tenderness, Rabelaisian as a friar and sensitive as a child, whom Verlaine described best as : 'Vif comme les pinsons, et mélodieux comme les rossignols.'

Coming late, at least as a professional musician, into the musical arena, Chabrier never quite acquired that independence and ease of style which gives the most commonplace of hack composers the text-book discipline of his time. The intermittent instruction of various masters, among whom the best qualified seem to have been Hignard and

Édouard Wolff, gave him a good enough grounding in the rudiments of his art, but in the superficial manner which his first compositions show. These were, moreover, amateur efforts which never pretended to do more than amuse a circle of uncritical friends, and aimed no higher than to reproduce the style of Hervé or Offenbach. Actually by the time he had reached the age of thirty, and under the influence of Wagner, he had built up for himself an individual idiom, and it seems that it was due more to the passionate study of great works of art than to the reading of text-books.

However ardent and keen his study, it had nevertheless not yet been sufficient to polish his method, and some of the letters published by Robert Brussel contain a frank statement of his preoccupation with technique, mentioning with an almost agonized urgency the difficulty he had in giving form to his thoughts. One comes across pathetic phrases of which the following is typical: 'Everything is a great effort to me. I must say I don't seem to have any facility.' (From a letter to Lacome, 1886.) And this seems to fit in with the opinion of Jean Chantavoine, who assigns this difficulty of writing, which appears in Chabrier's work sometimes by definite gaucheries, and sometimes by the too meticulous care over a phrase, not only to insufficient grounding but also to an innate quality of his nature. Reynaldo Hahn, an excellent critic of Chabrier's work and its multifold fecundity, accurately defines the defects in his technique by the remark: 'He tries to put in too much—he over-

crowds his canvas.' And speaking of Chabrier's
habit of writing his scores in pencil, he recalls his
resigned comment that it was easier then to add or to
rub out. 'The conclusion we are forced to', adds
Reynaldo Hahn, 'is that he erased one note to put in
two more.' But this is jumping to a rash generaliza-
tion. It is true that he often delighted in massing up
tonal texture, in thickening the harmonic background; and Legrand-Chabrier holds that his natural
gift only showed itself by what he added and not by
what he cut out. But all these devices, by which
Chabrier creates the illusion of skilfully conducted
revision, really never spoil his work except in his
ambitious dramatic compositions like *Gwendoline* and
Briséis. Here we see him trying to change his manner
without adequate training, entering the realm of the
symbolical and legendary, like d'Indy or Chausson, for
instance, and trying to express it. But he had not had
time to divest himself of his instinctive feeling for the
easily picturesque, for what is simply felt and clearly
definable, and mere tricks of style could not effect the
change and alter the irrepressible, familiar, and delightful facility of his melodic line into what he called
'grande musique'.

At the piano it was an entirely different matter.
No sense of constraint, no preconceived forms, no
grandiose tradition that he was struggling to comply
with. There we see the composer completely himself; his gifts for improvisation and for impressionistic virtuosity combine to express his delightful
talent in the most natural manner possible. He
abandons himself to his imagination, irradiating

gaiety, tenderness and rapture. What seemed out of place, even trivial, in the grand style of opera, here is full of genial and individual flavour.

The warm freedom of rhythm takes in its easy stride the charming vulgarities of doubled melody, delights in the sensuous clashes of seconds, imposes a curious strength to the lush stretches of appoggiatura, and turns chords of the ninth into the frolics of a faun. Here is the real Chabrier; the man who unconsciously, and through sheer force of sincerity, was to leave an indelible imprint upon the music of our time, enrich it by a new language, and infuse into it joy and movement.

It would be useless to look for any traces of this personality in the piano works before 1870. Besides, they are either immature childish works, in the first place, or, later, between the ages of fourteen and twenty-two, the diversions of a student, according to the chronological plan of M. Georges Servières. I am indebted to Robert Brussel's kindness for the loan of three precious little manuscript collections which enable me to work back to this point and investigate Chabrier's musical gift from its infancy.

It would be out of place to speak of them here if one were only discussing their intrinsic value. But the real interest of these unformed sketches is that they are the outpourings of a soul in the cradle; they give us an inkling of the influences around him— his aesthetic *milieu*, and the type of model which this schoolboy of Ambert had to work on during his musical education.

It is a depressing vista which opens out before us.

Emmanuel Chabrier

The first manuscript contains a dozen odd pieces probably selected and written, except the last few, which are in Chabrier's hand, by some one closely associated—his father, mother, or professor; it dates from 1849, and is a record of young Emmanuel's effusions until 1855, between the ages of eight and fourteen. We have a full account of Chabrier's early masters, two Spaniards named Zaporta (not Saporta as is generally written) and Pitarch, from Joseph Désaymard, Chabrier's compatriot and a well-informed critic. One does not want to malign them, but it does seem from the choice of subjects in this infant prodigy's repertoire—and prodigy he certainly was at home—that the models set before him aimed no higher than the slack standards one would expect from brass band audiences at Clermont-Ferrand. We notice three polkas, and as many polka-mazurkas, a schottische, a valse, a redowa, two mazurkas, a varsoviana, a nocturne called *Un Ange au Ciel*, and another called *La Nuit*. The dances have similarly pretentious titles: *Les Bords de la Dore*, *Les Bords de l'Alma*, *Euphrasie*, *La Chute des Feuilles*, *L'Echo du Verger*. And all of them excessively commonplace and barren of musical ideas. On the first page of the book, however, is a quotation from J.-J. Rousseau which is worth remark in that it anticipates the technical ineptitude that later was to become a millstone around Chabrier's neck: 'Music is the art of combining sounds in a manner pleasant to the ear. This art becomes a science, and a very deep one, when one investigates the principles underlying this combination and the psychology of our reaction to it.'

French Piano Music

The other two little manuscripts are pocket size, like dictation exercise books, dating from 1858 and 1859. The first contains a piece of advice obviously from the pen of the giver: 'If an idea comes to you, whether it is in the street, in the dormitory, in the study, in the refectory, &c., put it down at once in this little note-book, in case you forget it.' The advice was followed by the young schoolboy, evidently, for the book opens with a piece in G major in two-four time, headed by this sentence, which reveals a great deal of his adolescent ambitions: 'This little piece could be the introduction and chorus at the beginning of an operetta (words to be found).' And later, after a scrap of recitative, a fresh note: 'One or two harmonic chords (*sic*), before the theme. They are not so easy to get.' Is this not already, in effect, a remark as discouraged as the one quoted at the beginning of this essay, from the pen of the mature Chabrier?

With the exception of an unfinished sketch of a violin piece, full of high-flown progressions, packed with tremoli, and written evidently for his third music-master, the Pole Tarnowski, melodic banalities blossom afresh in the second of these two books, falling over each other in inextricable confusion. An orgy of quadrilles, valses, polkas, and ritornelli, whose nature or purpose is underlined by indications of this kind: 'Lively', or 'Graceful return, on the held trill; the Lady pirouettes'. Clearly, in the mind of Chabrier the schoolboy, music was synonymous with operetta, and Euterpe's bay wreath flourished in the gardens of the Bal Mabille.

Even though in the 'snap' of a theme here and there the element of future vivacity can be detected, it is vulgarized by its commonplace context, and associated, literally and figuratively, with chords so banal and devices so meaningless that it is almost impossible to believe, as one turns over these immature pages, that they heralded the appearance of one of the most individual, most vitally original, musical temperaments of our time.

Among the works of the same date as these last two manuscript books, M. Servières notices a piece called *Le Scalp*, consisting of a Vivace, followed by an Allegretto in D major in two-four time; the autograph copy of this, dated January 1856, is in the Malherbe Collection. There is also in the collection a Valse, in manuscript, dated 'Op. 1, August 1857'; it was dedicated to Mlle Julia Jullien and bears the title of her Christian name.

M. Servières, who has had the chance of looking through it, describes it as being preceded by a sentimental introduction in E flat, in twelve-eight time, with a theme incorporated later in the valse as a cantabile subject, the whole thing working up to a brilliant conclusion in the fashion of the day.

Chabrier's first published work was a suite of Valses called *Souvenir de Brunehaut*, issued in 1862 by a publisher named Gambogi in the Boulevard Montmartre. The plates of this piece were destroyed in 1889 when the firm went out of business, and all trace of copies has disappeared. A similar fate would have overtaken the *Marche des Cipayes*, published in

1863 by the same firm (M. Martineau says 1860, but the exact date is immaterial), but after several reincarnations it came into the possession of the firm of Mackar and Noël and was republished. One's feeling on reading it is rather to regret such solicitude, for apart from its greater length this work differs little from the others just mentioned. A few scraps of counterpoint, amusing tricks in the accompaniment here and there, a frankly ludicrous effect of 'crossing hands', are all characteristic of Chabrier, but do not suffice to hide the emptiness of the whole. Some critics have spoken of this work as a deliberate parody, but I am sure that it is unconscious. Its construction is clumsy and unfinished, and the themes follow each other formlessly and uncontrasted. One of them seems to come from *Le Scalp*, the bizarre piece with the title 'à la Mayne-Reid', noted by M. Servières. Remembering his short description of it, I imagine this theme to be the middle theme in E major; it is much more in the spirit of comic opera than of an Oriental march. This suggestion consoles us for our lack of information as to the rest of the piece.

It is not until the *Impromptu* in C major, dedicated to Mme Édouard Manet, that we touch Chabrier's authentic pianistic technique. His biographers disagree now and then as to the date of this piece, which marks, significantly and beyond all doubt, the crystallization of an entirely personal style. M. Martineau dates it 1861, M. Georges Servières 1873. The former states that Mackar and Noël published it, the latter Heugel. The real truth is that the first performance of it was given by Camille Saint-Saëns at the Société Nationale de Musique on 27 January 1877, at the same time as a Prelude that defies identification but which may possibly be one that appears under another title in the suite *Pièces Pittoresques*; it is now published by Enoch.

The dedication alone is enough to make M. Servières's theory probable, apart from the unlikelihood of a sixteen years' delay between the composition and the performance of the work. I very much doubt that the friendship between Manet and Chabrier sprang up from the very moment of his arrival in Paris; for not till he had spent several months at the Lycée Saint-Louis and at the École de Droit, where he kept his terms, did he finally get his appointment, on 20 October 1861, on the staff of the Ministry of the Interior. It is inconceivable, too, that this work, so full of originality and of rhythmic and harmonic subtlety, should be contemporary with that clumsily moving, formless *Marche des Cipayes*.

A gap of ten years at least is implied in a difference as marked as that between these two pieces. And, moreover, these ten years must have industriously and intelligently spent. They were indeed; for without neglecting his administrative work—or rather, resigning himself to getting through it with as little trouble as possible—Chabrier started on a course of harmony and composition under Semet and Aristide Hignard (the former was professor at the Conservatoire, the latter, holder of the Prix de Rome and timpanist at the Opera, a musician dogged by ill luck, and composer of a melodramatic *Hamlet* in five acts after the style of Berlioz). He spent his evenings copying out the works of the masters, perfected his piano technique with Édouard Wolff (said to be a pupil of Chopin), even embarked on violin lessons with Richard Hammer, and more than all this actively associated himself with the 'Parnassien' movement in Paris, coming to it with all the enthusiasm of the novice and all his magnificent reserves of fresh native vigour.

He was drawn into friendship with most of the writers and artists in the vanguard of the movement, revelling, in their company, in a kind of musical authority which enchanted him and stimulated his ambition. He gave musical advice to Villiers de l'Isle-Adam, who was fired with the idea of setting Baudelaire to music. He collaborated with Verlaine, who provided him with operetta subjects, later immortalizing this association of fine wits in tender, sad verses:

Chabrier, nous faisions, un ami cher et moi,
Des paroles pour vous, qui leur donniez des ailes...

He used to visit various salons and literary back-shops. In a word he profited everywhere by what Joseph Désaymard terms 'Chabrier's Parisian phase', seeing in it the root cause of his artistic development.

The *Impromptu* is the reflection of this stage of his life. It is, admittedly, by no means perfect; the ease of expression reached in one or two of the *Pièces Pittoresques* or in the *Bourrée Fantasque* was not his straight away. But now already, in the texture of a fragrantly warm and piquant, seductive music, lies a quality, caught up in arresting harmonies, which is to become familiar to us, the turn of a falling phrase which heralds *Gwendoline* or *La Sulamite*, the leap of the deft progressions of the *Joyeuse Marche* and of the *Bourrée*, the swelling melodic curves of the *Île Heureuse*.

This is the true Chabrier, this is his very audacity, his zest and vigour. The butterfly has at last torn itself free from the chrysalis. His technique is liberated and supple, and ready for the still rarer felicities of the future.

Again, the *Impromptu* shows all the characteristics of his pianistic idiom. The form of the piece is entirely conventional, with a scholarly regard for form. Several bars of introduction, then the statement of the theme in two alternating phrases, one in the major, the other in the minor, on a rhythm with a slightly insouciant Spanish lilt. A second and livelier theme follows in the form of an air de ballet. Then an interlude, or slow trio, in A flat major, broken by the brisk play of a two-eight measure which returns twice in mocking contrast to the sentimental principal theme.

Finally the exposition is repeated entire with a languorous and exotic coda.

But while the form is based on the least revolutionary of principles, like all Chabrier's piano works, the instrumental and rhythmic technique is steeped in imaginative caprice. The entire range of the piano with every ounce of its picturesque tonal resources is deliberately employed to enhance the colour of a luminous and ethereal stretch of writing. Delicacy of nuance and colour contrast, characteristic indication of future works, are surprisingly subtly created; *rubato* lends his melody a pliant and sensuous curve.

One could be forgiven—and Chabrier would have borne me out—for pressing an analogy between the musical art which is individual to him and which we see first of all in the *Impromptu*, and the succulent art of a fine Midi cook. There you see the same respect for old-fashioned recipes, the same regard for the methods of simmering and slow cooking, but also the inborn gift for good flavouring, the shrewd, unerring instinct for that last-minute pinch of seasoning that brings out the savour of the most ordinary dish.

It is in such light touches that one has to look for the secret of the acutely sensuous pleasure in music that Chabrier's art communicates. His art, as Joseph Désaymard agrees, appeals to those people who relish a harmony on the emotional palate as the connoisseur tastes a fine wine or bites through the scented flesh of a peach. Following out the culinary metaphor at the risk of seeming irreverent, I would add that the imaginative wealth of detail, the ripe succulence of harmony, the thrill of an unexpected rhythmic turn, bear the same relation to his music as the spice in a ragout. They are not essentials, but they give it individuality.

Between the *Impromptu* and the *Pièces Pittoresques*, which follow immediately after in the list of his piano works, another interval of seven or eight years elapsed. The latter were published in March 1881 by Enoch. We know that the complete set was not written all at once, but that between times Chabrier had had two operettas performed—*L'Étoile* in 1877 and *Une Éducation Manquée* in 1879, and it is unlikely that he had busied himself with instrumental composition before the latter date, which also marks the time when he gave up his Government appointment. From this point began Chabrier's career as a professional musician. It left him with no more than a dozen years in which to perfect his art, and he was hampered by material difficulties and by the ill health of his wife. But those years were brightened, also, by the revelation of Wagnerism and the glory of the great orchestral works which illumined the daily round while he was producer and director of the choir, from 1881, at the Concerts Lamoureux. It was on 9 April of this same year that the *Pièces Pittoresques* were first heard at a concert of the Société Nationale de Musique. Not all of them were played, and the selection included the *Idylle*, *Improvisation*, *Danse Villageoise*, *Sous Bois*, *Menuet Pompeux*, and the *Scherzo-Valse*. Mlle Marie Poitevin was the pianist.

M. Paul Poujaud, so intimately associated with the musical renaissance in France since 1870, and from whom we are awaiting the critical survey that he alone can give, remembers a remark made after the concert by César Franck: 'We have just heard an amazing work. This music links up our time with Couperin and Rameau.'

French Piano Music

It was high praise, and, though one knows Franck was invariably generous, amply justified. If one thinks back into the period and recalls the type of French piano music then written, one realizes how and to what extent Chabrier's work would seem at once full of novelty and yet narrowly allied to a long vanished tradition. While preserving the convention of 'drawing-room' music, it rid the type of its pompous artificiality.

In place of the bravura of arpeggios, shakes, scale passages, and grace-notes, which were only a disguise covering poverty of musical ideas, Chabrier introduced the robust, wholesome poetry of free rhythm, the direct appeal of simple melody. The outdated ornament of a weak *cadenza*, of the invariable tremolo, saw itself replaced by a harmonious and subtle ornamentation. I have heard it said that the *Pièces Pittoresques* were thought out in terms of the orchestra. The same could be said of the piano compositions that followed them, for they are written with the same sort of technique and bear the same specific qualities. Chabrier's pianistic style was burdened with no useless virtuosity; the occasional flash of a turn, the stressed accent of a trill, a rocketing sequence, all these are only the pianistic parallel of symphonic effects. His style is equally animated throughout, fed by fluid and deft harmonies which outline the rhythmic scheme. Thanks to it, there has returned to the art of pianism vigour, grace, and classic delicacy, freed from the deplorable domination of the pianist-virtuoso with all its derogatory implications. From this point of view alone the ten pieces which form the suite of *Pièces Pittoresques* have done more to reinstate the piano in the general favour of musicians than the same number of years of written or verbal propaganda could have done. I will analyse the work in detail: its importance in the corpus of Chabrier's achievement is all-engrossing, for the variety of aspects in which it reveals to us his instrumental method.

Paysage is the title of the first piece. M. Désaymard sees here a spiritual state rather than a picturesque appellation: 'Mehr Empfindung als Malerei', as Beethoven had already said in describing the scene by the stream's edge. And without dreaming of establishing a parallel between the two works, one would nevertheless have to justify even the suggestion by maintaining that Chabrier's piece held an element of contemplation which for my part I cannot feel is there.

The opening theme in D flat major is given out as a unison in both hands, suggesting an easy, sauntering rhythm. A modulating phrase based on the repetition of the first two bars brings back the theme, broadened, in the left hand, with a warmly expressive melody in counterpoint in the right hand. The lively interlude cuts across the prevailing calm with a tremolo of repeated notes; it bears some sort of resemblance to the section of M. Vincent d'Indy's *Poème des Montagnes* called *Coup de Vent*. In conclusion, there is an entire restatement of the exposition. Altogether the piece seems to me more descriptive than contemplative, and therefore not analogous to the Beethoven manner, although it holds no definitely descriptive detail.

Over the second piece, called *Mélancolie*, I am entirely in agreement with M. Désaymard. Here the feeling is wholly subjective and the descriptive 'programme' has no part to play. A dreamy melody in the upper register of the piano is given, together with its accompaniment, to the right hand alone. The muted answer is in the same rhythm, oscillating between a bar of nine-eight and a bar of six-eight, murmured in the lower register by a unison for both hands, separated by an interval of two octaves. The question and answer are repeated twice in the same way. A delicate dialogue is now established, punctuated with slow syncopations which lull the whole piece into quietness before it resolves into one expressive concluding bar. The longing beauty of these few lines, and their rounded perfection, defy analysis. There throbs the hidden secret of a languorous autumn night, drenched with the perfume of late roses. And it exhibits at the same time such polish of style that the whole work is a masterpiece 'en petit'.

Third piece: *Tourbillon*. This shows us the violent, key-smashing Chabrier of history, immortalized in Detaille's sketch of him making the piano explode into wild notes that shatter walls and floor like a bursting shell. Debussy records a similar impression of an intimate occasion. One day he found Chabrier playing over to his publisher the idyllic wedding song from *Gwendoline*, and went away to tell Paul Dukas afterwards: 'The piano had to put up with a lot!' I have myself often played on an instrument he frequently used at Mme Ménard-Dorian's house.

Emmanuel Chabrier

Not only were the corners of several notes actually broken off, but the inside surface of the cover that comes down over the keys was literally scarred with scratches and gashes, evidence of fine hand-to-hand engagements. And at Ambert, his native town, they still remember his last visit, after which all the pianos in the district had to be sent to be repaired.[1]

But to return to the piece under discussion—a hurricane careering through four pages—we see him turning rhythms upside down, jumbling good and bad together, tattered bits of Schumann, scraps of Offenbach, reducing the panting piano to pulp with his short, thick, and incredibly nimble fingers. And this tornado is supposed, it appears, to be the portrait in music of the woman to whom it was dedicated.

The next piece, *Sous Bois*, is a glowing contrast; Chabrier's delicate lyricism takes an exquisite flight. It is full of the quiet rustling of stirring leaves, the play of light filtering through green shadow, the heavy murmur of the earth, the divine peace of trees sleeping under a summer sky. The piano seems to

---

[1] In reference to Chabrier's piano technique, I quote these two characteristic criticisms: 'This was no correct pianist, no nimble virtuoso, accustomed to technical difficulties. Oh, no! He was a devil that entered into the instrument' (Henry Bauer).

'He played the piano as no one had before him and as no one ever will again. The sight of Chabrier bearing down upon the puny instrument through a roomful of charming women, and playing *España* to the accompaniment of a fireworks display of snapping strings and broken keys, was something so irresistibly funny as to be almost epic' (Alfred Bruneau).

gather and transmute into tone this immobile, blessed quietness.

Hanging above a sustained, unmoving bass, rocking in whispered rhythm from tonic to dominant, quivering broken chords convey an impression of the vague melodic design which forms the only theme in the piece. Harmony alone varies, by subtle, pivoting progressions of augmented fifths and common chords.

Towards the middle of the piece there is a delicate piece of imitation in the octave, in the dominant key. Then the tonality of C major reappears and the exposition is repeated with hardly any change.

The fifth number, *Mauresque*, has a vaguely oriental flavour no more than hinted at in the bass rhythm of the first few bars—slightly reminiscent of the Nocturne of the *Suite Algérienne* of Saint-Saëns—and in the little venture into the Lydian mode in the opening melody in rising thirds. After this the piece takes on the style rather of a polonaise. Several months later, Chabrier was to cull from Spain a rather more accurate notion of the Moors and their music. This piece contents itself with the development of one theme and one rhythm, exceptional neither in treatment nor novelty of design.

The *Idylle* follows, the gem of the series. Chabrier gives as an expression indication: ' "Avec fraîcheur et naïveté" (With freshness and simplicity). I should prefer to add ' "Avec finesse et distinction" (With delicacy and distinction),' implying in no sense a contradiction. A chaste and tender melody floats

delicately upon a continual ripple of quavers. And
that is all. But it is a jewel of colourful ingenuity,
fluent, musical grace and refinement. The piece is
written throughout in three parts, a charming and
deliberate example of classic restraint. The upper
part alone is played legato, and the two others weave
below it a web of gossamer tone; it is seen, as it were,
silhouetted against a soft mist of sound.

At times the bass breaks off its *pizzicato* and
shades into a sensitive chromatic colour; at the
return of the exposition a fluttering of semiquavers
enlivens and renews the rhythm of the accompaniment. These are the only decorative additions to
this exquisite music, whose whole value lies in the
perfect purity of its outline, its refined poetic restraint.

The seventh number, *Danse villageoise*, has a solidity of movement and rhythm which brings back to
us, though in a slightly academic guise, Chabrier's full-
blooded provincial robustness. The piece is founded
on the contrast between a simple pastoral theme in
A minor, and a pleasant little trio in A major,
sophisticated and elaborated. There is to be observed in this strictly formal piece the use of the pre-
romantic Menuet or Scherzo; most of the other
pieces in the collection also show it, but in a less
formal manner. It was convenient to Chabrier
because it involved repetition rather than development, and he was ill at ease in the region of thematic
development and all it brought in its train. There lies
the really weak point of his musical art and technique.
This gift only, or this effort of concentration, was

lacking in order to make him a genius of the highest class, but either the one or the other was unhappily absent.

The *Improvisation* which follows reveals a Schumannesque trait in Chabrier's talent. It is to be found again in one or two of the big lyrical works, *Gwendoline*, *La Sulamite*, or *Briséis*, but with this exception it is quite foreign to his piano music. An urgently impassioned phrase leaps from the middle register of the instrument, fastens on the rhythm in a wild upward rush, then suddenly flags and drops like a wounded bird. A second figure attempts without success to rekindle the flame, but it is quelled by tranquil arpeggio chords. The two figures are used in glowing counterpoint to introduce the first theme on a dominant pedal, supported by a warm chromatic progression in the bass. An abrupt stop crystallizes its regained vigour, and the smooth opening chords form a quiet conclusion.

It is curious to find Chabrier using the method of thematic development in the very piece which one might imagine, from the title, could best dispense with it, especially after what I have just remarked about the difficulty or habitual distaste he experienced with it. For this *Improvisation* is built up like the first movement of a sonata. It is, moreover, a fine piece of writing, full of substance, and exhaustive in musical exuberance.

The last piece but one, *Menuet Pompeux*, does not, in spite of its title, succeed in evoking the courtly ceremonies of a past epoch. It strikes a popular, even a bourgeois, note, and it is heavy-shod sons of the soil who dance to its strongly-marked rhythms. The actual minuet section, in G minor, is for the main part written in an almost orchestral style. The trio in G major unites a charming musical design with the oddest rhythmic hesitation. The passage is punctuated with stops which evidently correspond with the ceremonious steps of the dance. But the impression that one takes away from this piece as a whole is one of a rather affected sentimentality alien to its proper character.

The brilliant *Scherzo-Valse* which closes the set fully justifies its popularity; it carries a fine musical freedom, and its thick full-bodied character gives it a picturesque warmth.

I have already suggested that Chabrier was thinking orchestrally when he wrote the *Pièces Pittoresques*. Under the title of *Suite Pastorale* he assembled from them an orchestral work consisting of the *Idylle*, the *Danse Villageoise*, *Sous Bois*, and the *Scherzo-Valse*. At the first performance, which took place on 4 November 1888, at the Concerts Populaires of Angers, the Scherzo-Valse was rechristened *Gigue*, a precise title which certainly fits the bounding opening rhythm. But this title is still not right, because Auvergne has nothing to do with the Highlands, and this note of excitable, passionate licence, the stirring of wild feet, this buoyant, restless health, comes straight from Auvergne. By contrast the interlude—or rather trio in valse form, if we go back to Chabrier's first title—with its low-pitched murmur, its light whisper of quivering notes that dies away every four bars on a caressing inflexion of an arrested dominant or tonic, seems more like an 'air de ballet' for some fairy frolic. There is nothing here more substantial or enduring than the flight of a bee sipping honey. And the difference of character gains still more from the delightful rhythmic contrast between the third section of the Scherzo and the second section of the Valse. A truncated return of the opening subject, a quick conclusion, and the suite is ended; it brings us, too, the surprising conclusion that, at heart, no one was more respectfully considerate of the established tradition of music than the man whose name has always been associated with a lawless independence.

The fact of César Franck's appreciation, which I have spoken of before, takes on a new significance in this light; in the construction of this set of pieces alone, we find the wild Chabrier content to use stereotypes which Haydn's contemporaries would have found adequate. Of course there is novelty, inventiveness, and originality as well, as I have already remarked, to be observed in the harmonic research, in the instrumental tone colour and above all in the rhythmic animation. But the statement is none the less true, and though it does not in any way diminish the value of a pianistic work which for fifty years has kept alive both the curiosity and interest of its interpreters, nevertheless it makes us realize the distance which separates that work from the two most significant piano compositions that Chabrier wrote: the *Valses Romantiques* and the *Bourrée Fantasque*.

Emmanuel Chabrier

Between the composition of the *Pièces Pittoresques* and the two works I have just mentioned occurred an event of little importance in itself, but of considerable interest as regards Chabrier's artistic development. During the autumn of 1882 he made a tour of Spain which enabled him, as he became aware of the subtle workings of Iberian rhythms, to liberate within himself the consciousness of his own authentic individuality.

Not even the influence of Wagner was to prove so important as this, vital though that was to his musical development, and borne out in all the works of his last period. The musical personality of Wagner effected on Chabrier's temperament an almost chemical reaction. He precipitated, as it were, the musical substance which his conscious enthusiasm urged him to assimilate and to absorb in his own nature. And what resulted was an indecisive effort to mix two aesthetic elements, the instinctive and the philosophical, both losing in the process something of their specific qualities.

With the Spanish influence it was something quite different. Instinctively an affinity was at once discovered, complete and deep-rooted; and what was already an unconscious aspiration in Chabrier's work found its conscious formulation there on the other side of the Pyrenees. To watch him observing ecstatically, in his letters, the beauty of the rhythms and the magic of the melodic curves, describing with a marvellous accuracy (writing to Édouard Moullé, from Grenada, in 1882) the complicated variety of steps accompanying the dances, raving over the supple movements in the melancholy frenzy of the Coplas, is enough to make one realize that from that time forward, in spite of apparently conflicting influences, his music was to carry indelibly the perfume of the southern inspiration exalted by Nietzsche and first conceived in music by Bizet.

The three *Valses Romantiques* for two pianos, published by Enoch in October 1883, that is to say, the same year as *España*, are surprising in their fresh inventiveness, not only with respect to the period in which they were actually composed. Like Édouard Lalo's *Namouna*, and for identical reasons, they might easily hold a place in a programme devoted to new French music. Since the *Pièces Pittoresques* Chabrier's musical capacity here seems to have grown, his rhythmic gift expanded, his technique become individual.

The initial impulse is no mere by-product of *joie de vivre*; the deliberate 'will to create' gradually takes the place of that bounding verve which in most of the previous works is the distinctive stamp of the composer of *L'Étoile*.

If I were to analyse this suite, which cannot be included in the literature for a single instrument, I should be going beyond the limits of my intention. But it is impossible to conceive of Chabrier's real individuality, of his multifold fecundity, to quote Reynaldo Hahn, while still remaining in ignorance of this music, where the ingenuity of pianistic technique is enhanced by the resource of a continuous dialogue between the two instruments and by an unbroken interchange and working out of ideas.

Emmanuel Chabrier

One is continually falling back on Robert Brussel when discussing Chabrier; he writes in a recent analysis: 'Each of these Valses is a portrait of a woman and each has its own character. One is tender, another is vivacious, the third almost passionate. And all hold an element of pungent satire.'

Chabrier himself, quite foreign to his usual custom, had shown some confidence in the success of this work. He writes to his friend Paul Lacome, speaking of the Valses: 'Do you know, I believe they will sell well. There is very little music for two pianos. The girls who play the piano seriously (need I say how plain they usually are) will be sure to ask for them. Oh! they'll soon calm down . . . when they've read them. . . .!'

The *Trois Valses* were given their first performance at the Société Nationale on 15 December 1883, by M. André Messager and the composer. They received an exceedingly warm reception, more than justifying Chabrier's whimsical expectations.

Apart from the themes which he used in *España*, Chabrier had brought back from his trip to Andalusia a big harvest of local idioms with which he experimented freely in the improvising that delighted his intimate friends. One of them was the excuse for a *Habanera* that Enoch published in October 1885. This is a commonplace work whose character is either popular or simply trite, one does not know which. The pleasing counterpoint which adorns it at the return of the theme in the original key cannot succeed in sustaining any interest in this piece of casino music. I should not mention it but for its doubtful merit of having anticipated the countless Tangos which for some years accompanied the contortions of our contemporaries. Chabrier obviously thought otherwise, since he orchestrated this *Habanera* on the occasion of a concert of his compositions given on 4 November 1888 at Angers. In the years that followed the publication of the *Valses Romantiques*, with the exception of the worthless piece I have just mentioned, he gave himself up to dramatic composition and put instrumental works on one side. *Gwendoline* and the *Roi malgré lui* are milestones on his unlucky road towards those ambitions that he always hoped would materialize. On his way he added many songs to his output, among them those of that justly famous suite in which he anticipates Ravel and the *Histoires Naturelles* by entering with a humorous zest that has never been equalled on a description of the lowly poultry and of the pig dear to gastronomic experts.

Then, in 1891, Enoch published the *Bourrée Fantasque*, dedicated to Édouard Risler, and the last work published during his lifetime. Because of a close intimacy, on many grounds, with the man to whom this work is dedicated, then in all the glory of his young genius, and almost the only pianist of his generation that Chabrier tolerated, I am able to quote Chabrier's own views on the playing of his music.

He adhered, apparently, to meticulous detail of tempo and accent; Paul Dukas and Ravel, in our generation, have the same legitimate strictness. He insisted on the full value of a sforzando, he would not allow a forte to become a fortissimo, nor a diminuendo meant to establish a piano to vanish in a pianissimo. In the same way he maintained the fine difference between a ritenuto and a rallentando, and would not allow one to be taken for the other. He was rigidly insistent on the simultaneous attack by both hands, and all expression and tempo indications provided him with an endless stream of suggestions. He reveals his point of view in a letter written to Charles Lecocq in the same year as the publication of the *Bourrée*, in which he complains bitterly of composers who leave their works without the expression marks with which he himself was so lavish, as: 'Slovenly workers who don't take the trouble to clean up their scores, symphonies, and other works of art.'

I have already spoken of this exceptional regard for exact indication in reference to his early works. I am sure that it ought to be the first consideration of the player anxious to interpret Chabrier's music according to the composer's intention. The title of *Bourrée Fantasque* does not quite define this intention. *Bourrée*, certainly; the principal theme brings out the necessary traditional rhythm and hearty rustic breadth; but how are we to fit in with it, as its natural complement, the tender phrase which forms the second section of the piece, expressing itself in a winding, inconclusive spiral of sound? And if it is to be described as *fantasque*, surely there should be allowed in its execution a little of the freedom which we have just seen deprecated by the person best qualified to know?

French Piano Music

M. Désaymard, in other respects so well versed in Chabrier's point of view, tries to read into this work a romantic, almost a macabre element which in my opinion seems out of keeping with it; here I am sharing M. Servières's view. And I only take as a joke M. Chantavoine's remark that this title of *Bourrée Fantasque* appears to be intentionally designed to show the association of the individual with the racial aspect of Chabrier's artistic make-up.

Taking the music as it stands, then, there remains to be said that it is a lively and picturesque piece in duple time and based on two themes; it is clearly the most significant revelation of Chabrier's pianistic work, and its prefatory expression mark, 'Très animé et avec beaucoup d'entrain', gives us a sufficiently accurate clue to its character.

The very simple musical form works out according to the usual method of the *Pièces Pittoresques*. A short, ostinato rhythm of repeated notes comes out into the open, as it were, in the piano's middle register. It reappears in variation, without losing its defined, bounding movement, through a series of repeats which show it at varying pitch and under different forms. This exposition, in C minor, lively and concise, is brought to a sudden halt on an unexpected F sharp, where the second theme appears, a melodic slide of consecutive fifths working its way into the musical design and bringing a lyrical element into the piece as it broadens out. The balance of the piece is entirely maintained by the juxtaposition of these two themes in modification, in contrast, and by the deliberate use of ingenious combinations which divide or unite them in the service of a sparkling pianistic *tour de force*.

This work is full of rich detail and picturesque effect. No one had ever before written for the piano in this way, using unsuspected orchestral resources, exploiting timbres to stress rhythms, and all the brilliant impressionist possibilities of the pedal. This short *divertissement* for the piano set composers on the track of a new technique of musical tone colour; it was as significant as *España*, if not more so, and its revelation extended beyond France. Albeniz and Granados remember it in their most Spanish works; Rimsky-Korsakof, original as he was, bears traces of it in the *Coq d'Or*, and Stravinsky in *Petrushka*.

A work of this nature demands an orchestral transcription. In scoring it, working closely to the original text, Felix Mottl only did what Chabrier intended to do. The latter intimated as much in a letter of 6 September 1891, as well as his idea of arranging it for two pianos. Édouard Risler finally realized this last intention, when ill health interrupted all Chabrier's activities. His reason gave way at a critical moment, that for some time had been expected owing to an extraordinary state of mental over-excitement, soon after the publication of the *Bourrée Fantasque* in the spring of 1892. He died in September 1894, having grasped nothing of the ovation he received at the first performance of *Gwendoline* in Paris in 1893—when in his box at the Opéra he was a lamentably uncomprehending figure— and leaving *Briséis*, which he started with splendid vigour, unfinished.

French Piano Music

The few piano pieces which complete his work, and which I have not yet mentioned, are all posthumous.

The five pieces published in 1897 by the firm of Enoch, supplied with titles and dedications by the publishers, show evidences of having been composed about 1890. M. Martineau states that they are contemporaneous with the *Bourrée Fantasque*.

The *Aubade* is delicate and refined, enlivened by a rhythm which reminds one of a similar melody in the 'animal' suite; it alternates between an ironic figure—a mixture of *pizzicato* and percussion—later made expressive by a soft nuance of chromatic thirds, and a second figure with remote harmonies, instinct with a more definite lyrical freedom than hitherto to be found in Chabrier's work.

The *Ballabile* is akin to the trio of the *Scherzo-Valse* both in method and in character, based only on the light fluctuations of the initial theme. A languorous Coda brings a slackening of pace without altering the line of the melody, enhanced by soft harmonies.

The title of the *Caprice* is about as inappropriate as it could be for what is a maudlin hotch-potch of the sentiments of Tristan and Louis-Philippe; it was composed, I believe, on the occasion of a sight-reading competition at a provincial conservatoire. It opens with a slow carillon linked foolishly to an introduction which leads nowhere. For it is impossible to detect even the germ of a ballad tune in the few hopelessly old-fashioned bars which form the centre of this unsatisfactory sketch. But to make good this deficiency we have the charming *Feuillet d'Album*, which bears this deftly suggestive indication: 'En un mouvement assez lent de valse—et très tendrement.' A line or two of shivering longing, a dreamy languor, a Schumannesque evening shadow evoked from a smart casino terrace. Finally, to complete the collection, there is a *Ronde Champêtre*, written in clear-cut couplets to neat quick rhythms; its pleasant gaiety is accompanied by a discreetly old-fashioned refrain in the minor. It is a delicate piece of work, pleasing in feeling and classical in form, and here once more, from the other side of the veil, Chabrier reveals his unsuspected taste for moderation and balance. Robert Brussel observes that the second theme of this piece comes from an unfinished and unpublished operetta called *Fich-ton-Kan*, written in 1865 in collaboration with a librettist whom one would never guess from such a title—no other than Verlaine. With the exception of the so-called *Caprice*, which it would be best to leave in oblivion, these pieces as a whole are worthy of an honourable place among Chabrier's work. Even if we cannot find, comparing them with the *Pièces Pittoresques*, the lyrical perfection of a composition like the *Idylle*, or if we miss the fine pastoral touch of *Sous Bois*, and the contemplative quality of *Mélancolie*, we can, on the other hand, discern in the polish of careful writing a more discriminating Chabrier, surer of his technique, and even, in the etymological derivation of the word, more artistic.

Three pieces from this suite, *Ballabile*, *Feuillet d'Album*, and *Ronde Champêtre*, were given their first performance at the Société Nationale by Édouard Risler on 3 April 1897.

I prefer to pass over without mention the two posthumous pieces that the firm of Costallat has thought it a duty to publish. One of them, loosely called *Air de Ballet*, would defame the reputation of the most commonplace of composers. The other, *Capriccio*, was probably a sketch for the *Valses Romantiques*, dated 1883 and quite rightly since discarded by the composer; it was 'finished' by Maurice Le Boucher in 1914. We talk about the art of dishing up odds and ends; but this is a difficult and thankless task. A *Cortège Burlesque* for four hands, also posthumous and published by the same firm, is not worth mentioning except as documentary evidence.

There remains for me to speak of two pieces which appear in catalogues only under the titles 'transcriptions', and yet deserve our attention on various other counts. The first, *Joyeuse Marche*, was conceived and composed in the first place as a piano piece, although the Enoch edition labels it as 'transcribed for two hands by the composer'. It was, on the contrary, the reverse that happened, and the orchestral score was taken from this piano version. If it is true that Chabrier meant to produce this work in orchestral garb at Angers in 1888 under the title of *Marche Française*, then in Paris at the Lamoureux concerts in 1890 with its final title, it is none the less clear that this pseudo-transcription has all the value of an original, and that the warm robustness, the irrepressible verve and flow of this carnival rhapsody, is as unmistakable here as in the orchestral adaptation.

It must, moreover, be remembered that Chabrier always composed at the piano, and experimented there with combinations of timbres. So that it is hardly surprising to meet the same effects in the piano transcription which in the orchestral score underline the rollicking quality of its themes. The impudent grace-notes, the glissando scales, the rumblings which remind one of bassoons at play, the crashing of the palm of the hand in the lower registers, all make up a tone comedy, a Shrove Tuesday procession, as Chéret shows us on the delightful covers of its first editions. And it all ripples on in an irresistible flow, with an inimitable sensuous rhythm, while the counterpoint is cutting its own amusing little capers. This buffoonery belongs only to Chabrier. Neither Hervé nor Offenbach could have achieved such farcical parodying, which springs from the music itself, from the breaking up of rhythm and from a sort of harmonic comic sense which could make a joke out of an aptly placed six-four chord. Joseph Désaymard asserts that the ideal type of humorous music is a composition which is amusing without losing caste, without falling below the ideal of nobility expected from more serious works. I do not pretend that the *Joyeuse Marche* belongs entirely to this class. More ambitious examples achieve it, *L'Apprenti Sorcier*, for instance, or *Till Eulenspiegel*. But in the literature of piano music I know of no single piece which can be compared to this for vivacity of humour, comic

relief, and ironic use of instrumental resource, nor
one which imposes its wit upon so delicate a musical
quality. In claiming for the *Joyeuse Marche* its rightful
place in Chabrier's piano works, I am not so much
impelled by the need for exact classification as by the
desire to add, to the repertoire of those who interpret
this master of musical humour, a work whose
burlesque character has hitherto been missed.

The second transcription that I am anxious to
mention, Camille Chevillard's version of *España*, has
at least the virtue of having been made under the
composer's eye, though not written actually by him.
It can therefore be asserted that nothing appears in it
which Chabrier himself did not either suggest or
approve. He had played *España* on the piano too
many times on private occasions to allow the publication of a different version from his own. Moreover,
he had made an arrangement for two pianos from
the orchestral score, which Chevillard certainly used.
His transcription is in other respects very remarkable
and condenses within it all the orchestral effects. It
is called a 'transcription de concert', but perhaps that
is merely to distinguish it from Waldteufel's popular arrangement, that portentous suite of valses
which vulgarizes Chabrier's rhapsodic strength in
every sense of the word.

With due regard for proportion, and of course in
an entirely different spirit of buffoonery, Chabrier
himself was guilty of a musical solecism as bad as
Waldteufel's, but without dreaming either of making
money out of it, it is true, or of ever publishing it.

The case in point was the quadrille for four hands

Emmanuel Chabrier

called *Souvenirs de Munich, sur les thèmes favoris de Tristan et Iseult,* and dedicated to 'Monsieur Lascoux', a pompous police magistrate who for nearly half a century was one of the most uncompromising partisans in France of the Master of Bayreuth.

This dubious piece of jesting was conceived during the rehearsals of *Tristan* for the Lamoureux concerts, published first of all by the Revue S.I.M. in 1911, and recently issued for sale by Costallat, after having amused, *sub rosa,* a generation of hardened Wagnerites, who experienced a shocked delight at this disrespectful familiarity on the part of one of themselves, and only referred to it indirectly while gloating over it in secret like the memory of a great adventure.

The unveiling of the mystery is a disappointment even to those of us who remember that attitude and those old heroic days. And in re-reading this harmless little joke, a mosaic of glorious themes muffled up with titles like Poule, Pastourelle, or Pantalon—and even that does not succeed in making them ridiculous—one really begins to ask oneself if one is not rating the humour of Chabrier's work too high.

But even if it is revealed in his work with unusual richness, is this vivid sense of comedy whose incomparable secret I have supposed him to possess— once for all and without disputing it—really the chief reason for claiming our admiration? Is there not something more and better than this gift of comedy hidden beneath the negative virtues which I have heaped up over his memory? In the series of pieces that I have just analysed did I not say that the most precious and most individual were precisely those which abandon the spirit of easy exuberance for a purely musical sensitiveness? Burlesque is no motive for *España*, the *Bourrée Fantasque*, *Idylle*, *Sous Bois*, the *Valses Romantiques*, and the *Ode à la Musique*, to name only a few of the most remarkable of his works. Fancy is there, certainly, and lightness of touch. But they were also to be found in the music of Couperin, Rameau, and Haydn, without contemporary hearers dreaming of calling them comic composers. What the laughter of Silenus was must have been forgotten at the beginning of the third Republic if people could pretend to see nothing else in an output which was notable for introducing so many other new features.

Chabrier was little inclined to lose himself in contemplation, says M. Désaymard. Clearly so; and as Jean Chantavoine neatly put it, he entered into music by the gate of laughter. But the same writer still asks himself, as I do, whether this laughter does not hide a curious longing. Chabrier one day said to Paul Poujaud after listening to a performance of César Franck's quartet: 'That is the sort of music I should have liked to write.' This is just the music he could not write. But we can surely find in his rhythmic inventiveness, in his feeling for subtle harmonies, in the unexpected turn of his melodic gift, and above all in the broad exuberance of his manner, a contribution to music at least as striking as this comic gift which opened for him the portals of his career. 'I am cultivating the gift of gaiety,' said

Chabrier. And who would say that this was not deliberate? Vincent d'Indy speaks of his 'sensitive exuberance, the inherent quality of his talent, fundamental cause of the unfettered melodic expansion that makes his music so telling'. M. Martineau remarks that 'Emotion was for him the *raison d'être* of music'. I have in my hand, thanks to Robert Brussel, the scores of the Ring cycle, annotated by Chabrier when he was at Bayreuth, and it is interesting that only the deeply expressive passages are underlined with enthusiastic comments. And when, in the name of the Société Nationale de Musique, he spoke those touching words over the tomb of César Franck, one asked oneself, could they have been conceived in the mind of a musician who had not himself also tried to realize in his own work the true nobility and the true greatness of his art?

It is high time to assert that the reason for his influence on the generation of musicians that followed him and who have vindicated his memory is not entirely the spirit of light-hearted farce. And that if his influence has penetrated the musical art of our time and is daily increasing, it is because it bore a quality more enduring and convincing than laughter, even resounding laughter.

It is only just to the man who could write these anguished words: 'Never will there be an artist who has more loved and sought to do honour to music than I, no one will ever have suffered more for it—and I shall suffer everlastingly.'

V

The Piano Music of Paul Dukas

THERE are two works only, with the exception, that is to say, of the couple of short *pièces d'occasion*, which form a supplement, as it were, to Dukas's pianistic stock-in-trade, and which I am reserving for discussion till later on account of their peculiar nature. Two works only, but of primary interest, rich, concentrated, charged with musical breadth, full of care and thought. One of them, the Sonata, dates from 1900; the other, *Variations, Interlude et Finale sur un thème de J.-Ph. Rameau*, from 1903. Both are published by Durand.

These pieces are practically contemporary with *Ariane et Barbe-Bleue*, and follow, in the course of a life-work deliberately restricted by the desire always to achieve nothing but the best possible, the Overture to *Polyeucte*, the glorious Symphony in C, and *L'Apprenti Sorcier*, that brilliant tone poem which in the space of a few weeks gained for its youthful composer undying fame on both sides of the world.

The present essay was undertaken by no means for the precarious pleasure of mere aesthetic analysis. I am aware of the purely relative value of the analysis of a work of art, and it was observed not so long ago, in an attempt to estimate the value of similar studies, that 'The work itself is the best evidence of what one is trying to establish, that is, that it is a fine work'. But in publishing a few notes made originally for personal use, I feel I may perhaps help students in the

future by saving them trouble in some directions and
stimulating them in others. And so inspire them to
pay Dukas's work the compliment of giving it the
careful attention it deserves, or even demands.

The pages that follow will therefore be of interest
only if they are accompanied by the reading of the
musical text. I could have avoided this condition
by filling the pages with quotations in such number
that they would amount to the entire reproduction
of the pieces under discussion.

The Sonata is the earlier in date of the works to be
analysed and undoubtedly represents one of the most
serious attempts ever made to express the Beethoven
form in terms of French pianism.

This is not merely a similarity in form or technique, but in choice and type of themes, in the
method of the development, and in the beauty of a
lyrical feeling both condensed and brilliantly lucid;
as a whole it does approach the kind of sublime
expressive synthesis immortalized in Beethoven's
later sonatas and later quartets. It is constructed in
four movements, all deliberately separate and un-
bound by any cyclic association of ideas, although
M. d'Indy says exactly the opposite in his *Traité de
composition*. All the same, anxious though he clearly
is to find in Dukas's work a dependence on a factor
failing which, according to d'Indy and his school,
there was no salvation, he admits that this dependence is in the spirit rather than in the letter. And
this distinction is a little perverse, seeing that
M. d'Indy gives us no further explanation of what,

wishing to believe himself, he would like us to accept as a proved fact. I have tried in vain to find any trace of association, whether superficial or obscure, which could convince me of cyclic unity between the separate movements of the Sonata.

At the very most, there might be traced in the Scherzo a passing hint of the opening theme of the first movement, or in the introduction to the Finale, the clash, in altered rhythm, of two melodic figures, which are to be used again in the Finale itself. And this seems insufficient to justify the inclusion of the work, however flattering the implication, in a tradition which one supposes to be subject to the most rigid rules.

The only basis on which one can admit real association between the four movements of the Sonata is in a uniformly high level of idea and form. And I should really be at a loss to assess its virtues by the application of any test whatever of standardized musical style.

The first movement, bearing the tempo indication 'modérément vite', opens in an expressive vein created by the juxtaposition of two long melodic phrases which form the germ of its development. The first is melancholy, racked by insistent, dragging, syncopations, the second gives out a warm and expressive response. They unfold with a grave grandeur which beyond Beethoven and Franck seeks the secret of its power in the cantilena of Palestrina.

The melodic line is conceived, formed, and developed according to the demands of a strong logic

Paul Dukas

which cannot work itself out in a mere word or two.
And not only are the themes of equal importance
rhythmically, but they have a close common relation-
ship, in spite of their variety in type, which makes
them akin to the purest classical examples. Nevertheless, this apparently altogether traditional principle
does not disallow a fine audacity, a fine independence
of idea or execution.

It is here, in my opinion, that Dukas's striking individuality of talent shows itself. His learning and
his discrimination have taught him the value of
precedents whose aesthetic merit has stood the test
of centuries. But his deep-rooted individuality has
never been subordinated to the method used to
give it expression. It is constantly following a familiar course without in any way sacrificing its own
distinctive features. Jacques Rivière has often revealed genuine sincerity and a penetrating analytical
capacity in speaking of works which he admired, but
when he stigmatizes what he calls the frankness with
which Dukas's music is content to be unoriginal and
openly to declare its ancestry, I feel that his insight
has left him. I do not think I am wrong in saying
that Dukas embarked on the composition of the
Sonata in a spirit of instinctive revolt against the
tyranny of Wagnerism—the supreme menace of his
day to the individuality of composers. In the strict
convention of classical pattern he sought protection
from the pervasive influence whose effects he
dreaded. For this reason he draws near to Beethoven,
but is it not possible to see in this kinship and its
results a gesture of independence rather than a

merely docile imitation? We can, moreover, repeat in an analysis of Dukas the same words that he used to describe César Franck:

'It is because the idea is classic, that is to say, as universal in its range as possible, that it is clothed in classic form; not by reason of a conscious theory nor of a reactionary dogmatism that subordinates idea to form.'

Mlle Blanche Selva seems to have passed over this concise confession of faith when, in her book *The Sonata*, she analyses the progress of ideas in the first movement as follows:

'The first theme in E flat, then in A flat, moves towards D flat. This harmonic progression serves as a bridge passage to bring about a preliminary statement of the second theme, which appears in C flat, the subdominant of the key of G flat in which it is properly stated. An animated development, at first of the opening theme, later of the second unaltered. Ordinary recapitulation, but without the preliminary statement of the second theme; final development of the second theme with which the movement ends.'

These are actually the essential factors of this solidly built work, if reduced to a scheme. But though it is strictly correct, I find it a little misleading that Mlle Blanche Selva, who was the outstanding exponent of the Sonata of Paul Dukas, should find nothing to say about it beyond this tedious definition.

'Ni littérature, ni peinture', could be written above this work, as that meticulous composer, Gédalge, inscribed over his third symphony. Perhaps, but it is music, real music, that we are discussing and not a boring statistical pigeon-holing of radiant ideas in terms of cold-blooded calculation. This plan, this reasoned arrangement, taken as the substance of a musical work, conveys nothing of the emotional impulse of a musician's thought, communicating to us his anguish and his joy. It is, of course, an integral part of the work, for we cannot separate a lofty sentiment from its technical method of expression. But too often it happens that the latter is taken for the former, or worse, that the latter is assumed to be the only thing of importance. It results in subordinating all the magnificent freedom of musical creation —this 'written agony', as Chopin called it—to the painstaking mechanism of setting up, as it were, an accurate page. And certainly that is inadequate to demonstrate reasons why we should admire or cherish it. The Sonata of Dukas, fortunately, has rarer qualities than the mere disposition of themes or keys.

I have already mentioned the uneasy melancholy of the opening theme of this first movement. The effect is deepened still more by the pianistic method employed. The left hand, by continual crossings so technically difficult that their very appearance conveys, visually, the agonized quality of the theme, keeps the melody and the bass going at the same time; the melody is broken by expressive rests, which the right hand dramatically fills in by a rushing eddy of semiquavers.

Thirty-two bars of exposition, according to this invariable plan, give this prefatory passage time to disseminate its emotion and inspire the listener with a sensation of doubt or disquiet to which the second theme brings the solace of warm relief and buoyant rhythm.

The initial sense of uncertainty comes again to the fore in a curious questioning phrase emerging from the first theme, ritenuto, and a struggle is established between the melody which entreats and the melody which promises consolation.

The opposition of these two ideas gives birth to the dramatic atmosphere in which this first movement is steeped. An odd coincidence comes to light after the exposition, in a persistent upper pedal above the chromatic ascent of the bass, reminding one of an episode in Brahms's B minor Rhapsody, itself not unlike an equally famous passage from the duet from *Carmen*.

Then the second theme, melody of consolation, made still more subtly persuasive by the relaxing of rhythm in its accompaniment, which turns semiquavers into triplet quavers, is given a broad statement in imitation at the octave, in the translucent keys of B flat major and E major. The return in the bass of the opening semiquavers acts as a bridge passage to the return of the opening and its recapitulation, to which the second melody, in the key of E flat major, once more brings relief. The two themes are reunited in a coda full of ecstatic reconciliation. The theme of consolation floats for a second in the distance of an unexpected key change. Then, three ominous chords re-establish the restless tonality of E flat minor, leaving behind them, as it were, the shadow of mystery still unsolved.

We can agree with Mlle Selva that the second

movement, marked 'Calme, un peu lent', is in developed sonata form. That is, it employs two themes which move in the traditional way, the one establishing the principal key of the movement, A flat major, the second starting in the passing tonality of the dominant. There follows a development which in modulating phrases, but here without changing the prevailing unity of sentiment, reintroduces these two melodies, complementary rather than opposed. Finally, and still in accordance with sonata form, there is a recapitulation in the principal key.

A peculiar characteristic of this piece is the cumulative animation in the figures of accompaniment as they are unfolded about the melody in plastic counterpoint. In the *Arietta* of Beethoven's Op. 111 or in the *Aria* of César Franck, there are examples of a similarly deliberate use of decorative variation at the same time as the 'double' of the harpsichordists. The main theme at first appears in crotchets; a little before the entry of the second subject, quavers creep into the harmonies; then in the second subject itself and as far as the recapitulation, triplet quavers; and finally from the recapitulation to the coda, semiquavers in sextuplets.

The variety of these secondary rhythms, though in no way affecting the contemplative feeling of the piece, yet bestow upon it a kind of interior oscillation which acts as a foil to the untroubled peace of the melodic curve.

The involutions of pliant counterpoint, and its smooth progression, only serve to stress the slow quiet curves of the first theme, in a way almost to disembody it, though without taking from its colour. By contrast, they give to the tender ardour of the second theme a wealth of expression, by a subtle network of appoggiaturas and suspensions, like the persistent stirring of awakening life.

Is this a mood or a landscape, one wonders? The contemplation of a philosopher or a sentiment profoundly pastoral? In any case it is a magnificent piece, of exceptional musical content, with an element of repose accompanying its delicately restrained exuberance with true feeling.

In his monograph on Paul Dukas, Gustave Samazeuilh accurately observes that this piece constitutes a striking example of what breadth the quiet serenity of the Beethoven andante form can convey to the most advanced of modern feeling.

But, inspired by such a model, it is still urgently necessary not to content oneself with a mere copy of its exterior. I could not pay a greater tribute to Paul Dukas than to say that the depth and nobility of his inspiration more than justify Samazeuilh's comment.

The third movement of the Sonata, a scherzo form in duple time in B minor—a key taken enharmonically for C flat—has the picturesque appearance of a flying rush with both hands in defiance of pianistic obstacles, with the agitated crackle of alternating semiquavers punctuated at irregular intervals by quick, insistent accents. This restless fever acquires regained strength and vigour by the rhythmic vivacity of a complementary theme

Paul Dukas

which can be called the second subject of the scherzo. The obstinate rush of both hands is maintained, unyielding, until opposed by the inert resistance of long-drawn minims. It is at this point that we find the hint of the principal theme which, in spite of its episodic character here, induces M. d'Indy to class the work as cyclic.

The extension of note values makes way for the opening of a fugato interlude, involved and indeterminate, playing here the conventional part of the trio.

Mlle Selva gives this section an imaginative description which is in pleasant contrast to her analysis of the first movement:

'When the scherzo dies away in the gloom, the melody of the original figure takes its turn while the shadows gather until we are deep in a subterranean vault full of dim horrors, where spectres creep, formless, unsubstantial and nameless, struggling painfully to rise and falling in anguish back into the darkness.'

The nightmare effect of this sinister passage, though slightly lessened in the course of the episode by several bars of harmony which at once take away from its spectral character, is only dispersed finally by the return of the scherzo rhythm, bursting out at the very top of the piano in a shower of rapid notes.

The scherzo is repeated almost in its entirety, with a few changes of detail, up to the middle section, which serves as a coda, appearing this time in tremulously timid guise to the sustained beat of encircling semiquavers. There is a short break; then a curvetting phrase of four insistent notes breaks away in leaps, followed by a tentative reminder of the trio theme. A curious, single, held note arrests the attention for a moment, and then the whole fantasy vanishes on the turn of two ironic *pizzicati*.

The firm definition of the themes in this piece is a familiar trait in Dukas's work. *L'Apprenti Sorcier* had already afforded characteristic examples. In one of the articles he devoted to his friend's Sonata just after its brilliant first performance, Debussy says that hidden beneath the picturesque surface of this scherzo 'is a power that directs its rhythmic fancy with the silent steely force of a machine'.

The remark is perfectly apt, and it is also the distinguishing mark of Maurice Ravel's *Scarbo* which appeared several years later, revealing the most surprising and varied inventive vigour within the strict bounds of a classically formal scheme.

It is a characteristically French method, and yet not without a remotely Mendelssohnian quality. Again, certain technical pianistic devices of the Leipzig master find an unconscious but remarkable analogy in the construction of the scherzo of Dukas, at least in the opening section.

Another influence, and one asserted more in the spirit than in the letter, to use M. d'Indy's specious distinction, is that of Beethoven; it is revealed in the notable use of a fugato style in the interlude. We glimpse it again in the opening of the introduction to the Finale, where, as in the introduction to the Fugue in Beethoven's Op. 106, the creative impulse seems to hesitate between various

Paul Dukas

themes, making even its own indecision an excuse
for an expressive stretch of writing, and not finally
coming to a decision until the exposition of the
Finale proper.

The melodic elements of the concluding movement are all to be found here, but in a fragmentary,
rather showy form, shorn of the firm rhythmic insistence which, later, gives them a sturdy vigour.

The first notes of the introduction are no other
than the opening notes of the trio in the scherzo
inverted—if this kind of musical puzzle is of any
interest—taken, as it were, the wrong way of the
grain, and changed in character as much as in actual
disposition, from seeming sinister and foreboding to
a masterful and imperious mood. Little by little, after
attempting various melodies quickly discarded, the
composer's idea seems to crystallize, focusing on the
opening phrase of one of the themes previously given
out. It is sustained in an increasingly marked rhythm
to a point where, at last freed from indecision, it is
given out 'sans hâte et bien scandé', ushering in the
magnificent last movement which crowns the whole
work.

We find, again, in this last movement the bithe-
matic sonata form which served strictly for the first
movement and with a certain modification for the
second. But it is shown here to be of an unusually
complex mechanism, owing to the presence of
fragmentary figures in each of the main themes—
fractional themes, as it were, each giving rise to distinct development on its own.

The first theme is formed by two heavily syncopated phrases, the second more exuberantly lyrical than the first. The second theme is similarly divided into two phrases linked by a kind of *divertissement* which calls the first and anticipates the second. The first half of this second theme bears a grave richness, almost liturgical in cast, as M. d'Indy rightly notices in deriving it closely from the Pange Lingua plain-chant. One cannot forget, too, the fine use that M. d'Indy has himself made of this theme in the climax of *Fervaal*. Dukas's theme, at least in its prevailing feeling, might be compared with equal justice to the broad D major theme in triple time in the Sonata of Liszt. The second phrase carries with it a mood of lofty pride, adding an element of chivalry and a streak of romance to the clash of feeling involved at the close of the movement by these four motifs of entirely different character.

A little before the recapitulation, the principal subject of the Introduction, broadened and sonorous, brings the development to its climax, introducing a prophetic note in the richly varied play of parts.

The recapitulation itself clears the ground for a tonal display of almost orchestral dimensions, achieved by a still further elaborated instrumental technique. All the themes of the Finale reappear in full force, preserving their original identities with a redoubled ardour and renewed exaltation, in an atmosphere of apocalyptic fervour. A vigorous coda concludes this feat of creative energy, in which is revealed the finest of musical intelligence placed at the service of the noblest of inspiration.

Paul Dukas

I have several times remarked on the Beethoven quality of style in this monumental work, and it is worth stressing, because we shall discover in it something more than a deliberate choice of musical technique. This lofty disregard for modern influences is by no means to be interpreted as a mere reverence for the past. It is the sign manual of a forceful personality which finds no other instruments strong enough to chisel out his mighty conceptions but the tools of his ancestors, and simply resharpens them for his own use.

By contrast with the imponderable, expressive music of Debussy, full of subtle evasions, creating the magic of his art through the actual sensuous beauty of his style, and opening up new vistas of tonal poetry for the piano, the art of Paul Dukas seems direct, virile, without artifice. In his work he is not concerned with piano technique for its own sake; it is the means to the end of musical expression, not an end in itself. In the Sonata ingenious detail is used only to strengthen and enrich the course of musical development; it is embodied in it without extraneous decorations of any kind, scorning virtuosity that does not directly enhance the underlying musical ideas.

His piano technique is sometimes a little ponderous and overloaded; for that very reason it is the best possible medium for expressing the titanic character of some of the themes, particularly in the first movement and in the finale.

It is no use looking here for grace of ornament or wit; his art is not intended 'ad usum solistae'. Its musical eloquence is expressed by the most direct of methods, by plain harmony, rhythm, counterpoint. It sometimes goes beyond the tonal resources of the piano, if not the capacity of the pianist, and throughout it demands from the latter the full use of ten fingers resolved not to squander their strength. But he does disregard grace of effect, and so far from making any effort to lend charm to the music he has conceived, his impulse is in the opposite direction, tending to wrap it up in profound abstraction, to concentrate rather on its shadows than on its high lights.

This finely deliberate work draws on philosophical resources of unusual depth. It consequently loses —and perhaps it is not a great loss—the interest of the average listener who, in enjoying a musical work, is unused to giving it as close attention as if he were playing it. In the first of the two articles that Debussy wrote on the Sonata of Dukas—and both of them are oddly constrained and unenthusiastic, in spite of the high regard he professed for the composer—he supports my impression on this point:

'The sort of sealed emotion which is expressed there, and the fettered reticence of development demand unquestionably a deep intimacy with the work. . . . It is the outcome of an inexhaustible patience in adjusting its fine mechanism, and it is doubtful whether one could follow the course of the work at a concert performance.'

To which Dukas could have answered, in anticipation of André Gide, and with the same justifiable arrogance: 'I do not write to be read, but to be re-read.'

Paul Dukas

Besides, it has been proved by actual instances that even the listener who is utterly indifferent to matters of musical technique cannot escape being impressed by the grandeur of this work, by its powerful, broad proportions and its immense poise.

The first hearing of the Sonata was given by Risler at the Salle Pleyel on 10 May 1901, in the course of a concert at which I had the privilege of playing with him a number of pieces for two pianos. Both the work and its interpreter had a great reception, confirmed enthusiastically by the critics, with one or two negligible exceptions. Pierre Lalo, in particular, gave it a striking article in *Le Temps*, citing it as a landmark in the history of French music.

It was this that evoked Debussy's second article, to which I have already alluded. In the satirical commentary of 'M. Croche, anti-dilettante', it is no use whatever trying to find any other motive than a carping desire to oppose the opinion of the Schola, of which, rightly or wrongly, M. Lalo was supposed to be the mouthpiece. When we find him accusing the latter of preferring the substantial merits in the Sonata of Dukas to the expressive delicacy of the Sonatas of Chopin and Schumann, we know very well who he is up against, and that the work of Dukas is only the excuse for a quarrel on a point of principle. Later on he scoffs at the mention of the prevailing influence of Beethoven, to whom Pierre Lalo had naturally turned in his effort to define the unusually noble quality of the work he was analysing. One observes reading through these pages that others besides Debussy have yielded to the same inclination. Whether or not it is true, Debussy asserts that he would have hardly been flattered by the comparison if he were in the place of his friend Dukas, and gives this surprising reason : 'It is', he says, 'that the Beethoven sonatas are very badly written for the piano.'

Saint-Saëns, to whom the work is dedicated, never even acknowledged the receipt of it, I believe. I suppose this can be taken as an opinion, if necessary. But it has not prevented another one—what we call public opinion—from setting this magnificent creation that is Dukas's Sonata at the head of the permanent achievements that the French school has contributed to the glory of the piano.

The *Variations, Interlude et Finale sur un thème de Rameau* reveal a slightly different aspect of Dukas's pianistic style. The work was composed only a month or two later than the Sonata and heard for the first time at the Société Nationale on 23 March 1903, when Édouard Risler again had the privilege of being its original interpreter.

It is not that one can formulate a definite change in the quality of musical ideas. Beneath the daring metamorphosis of the innocent little theme which forms the foundation of this substantial work we find again that freedom of design and warm strength of rhythm that in themselves make for the creation of the right effect as it were, kindling vivid phrases that fix themselves in the memory at first hearing; qualities so satisfying that the listener wonders why such lucid and individual outlines are not always to be found in the art of music.

But in Dukas's method of expression is a definite change, though I would not dare to call it an advance. It shows itself in more subtle use of the instrument, a more colourful technique than the austere mechanism of the Sonata displays; in a more delicate and ethereal style, in the increased variety and rarity of his harmonic idiom, subtly and seductively enriched.

The conclusion is not to be drawn that the artistic value of the Variations depends only on technical skill in construction. The dexterous originality of the composer is here seen grappling with a most difficult problem, and M. d'Indy can well say that his work is a real synthesis of the three forms of variation: ornament, decoration, and development. But even the perfect balance exhibited between matter and form is enough to justify a preference for it from the point of view of objective aesthetics, and to establish its superiority. Once again—and may Debussy forgive me—Dukas found initial inspiration in the great example of Beethoven, in that pinnacle of his art and knowledge, the thirty-three amazing variations written round a commonplace Diabelli valse.

The plan and character of the two works are certainly different, but they are the outcome of a similar method. It can be formulated thus: given a basic theme, to draw from it musical ideas which best enable one to forget it. This is by no means the ordinary definition of the form, it must be admitted. But while Beethoven in a mood of exasperation followed this *divertissement* through and produced a masterpiece, the capricious paradox of a genius amusing himself by annihilating a banal melody with blow after blow of sheer inspiration, Dukas, on the contrary, had no intention except to glorify, to canonize a memory, to reveal his artistic parenthood. One recalls the 'affaire Rameau' in Paris at the beginning of the twentieth century, and how in this momentary lapse into the old 'guerre des Bouffons', Dukas, Debussy, d'Indy, and others of our greater musicians, all took the side of the old master.

Even though Dukas calls his work: *Variations sur un thème de Rameau*, it would be more correct to call it *Variations selon l'esprit de Rameau*. For though the theme selected, a minuet from the fourth Suite of *Pièces de clavecin*, has a desultory charm and a certain grace, it is not a notable instance of the sound style nor of the lovely crystalline inventiveness that we are accustomed to find in the works of the father of French music; these nevertheless are the very qualities—lucid principles of balance and logic—that Dukas reveals in this piece in which he consecrates himself entirely to the glorification of a great memory. And it seems to me that it is in this way we must interpret his impulse and his intended tribute. For, as we see, his finely conceived music, in rising higher than its source, had no other end in view than to throw up in better relief this framework of two or three insignificant bars which served as its inspiration.

Rameau's contemporaries had already long ago dubbed these sixteen bars with the nickname under

Paul Dukas

which the piece has come down to us, 'Le Lardon'. It was a burlesque description of the action of one finger of the left hand as it interjected a series of detached notes between the fingers of the right hand—suggestive of a chef running strips of fat through a joint.

This little minuet won an easy popularity in its day as much for this odd characteristic as for its extreme simplicity and its pleasant dance rhythm—a popularity probably disproportionate to its real merit. At any rate, there seems to be no striking originality about it that would naturally earn for it the privilege of inspiring one of the most notable piano works of our time. And again, its limitation of key imposes a constraint from which it would seem difficult to free oneself, and offers no scope for enterprise or variation. For in this sustained D major the only variety is a tentative hint of the dominant in the course of the second repetition, followed by the flash of a subdominant in preparation for the final cadence.

We shall see with what inventive fertility Dukas turns this theme to account while seeming to ignore it.

The following is the formal scheme of the work according to M. Vincent d'Indy's analysis of it in his *Traité de composition*:

'The theme is variously treated in eleven variations, and then, after a broadly developed episode in which the various points in the twelfth variation are sketched in, the twelfth variation, which forms the Finale, opens in a robust, vivacious manner, which reaches in an immense climax the Rameau theme that here appears, as it were, amplified to the giant proportions of the work of which it has just supplied the decorative subject.'

If we go on a little ahead into detailed discussion, we notice, apart from the divisions just indicated in broad lines and implied by the actual title, the presence of three distinct contrasting groups, in the Variations proper, that is to say, before the Interlude. The first group, in which the melodic character of the theme is more specifically maintained, includes the first six variations; the second group fastens on the rhythmic interest, and covers the next four; and the eleventh variation serves, as it were, as a preparation for the Interlude, and anticipates its improvisational character. The arrangement is not new, and we could find instances of this division into contrasting sections in most big works in variation form; it lessens the unavoidable impression of monotony due to the too frequent repetition, rather than the development, of an underlying single theme. But here the musical scheme acquires unusual flexibility and variety by the skilful interweaving of a supplementary idea.

Each of the variations which form these groups has for its base a different fraction of the theme and not the theme itself. The generative element is a melodic figure of three or four notes, perhaps, or a characteristic rhythmic turn. If one may use the word 'cellular' without undue pedantry, it describes better than any other this particular kind of constructional technique.

The problem for the interpreter involves some effort of mind, even to those most deeply versed in the science of musical sound : to isolate these musical embryos and identify them in fragments of the theme and then follow out their transformations. But the reward which awaits them is ample recompense for their trouble. I would say further that they will be amazed that such apparently fussy and meticulous adjustment of musical apparatus should have consequences so entirely unforeseen, whether in the astonishing freedom of their expression or in the eloquent breadth of the development they entail.

I do not feel that it is out of place to analyse this work variation by variation, and so to identify the relation of each one, whether close or distant, with the main theme. It must be borne in mind that this is composed of two eight-bar phrases, which for the convenience of analysis I shall refer to as the first and second sections.

Variation I, in D major, 3/4. In the character of an expressive dialogue in four-part writing. The highest part gives out a melody which contains, adorned with suspensions and appoggiaturas, the essential notes of the theme, which the bass similarly gives, with various free ornaments in the outside notes of the left hand.

Variation II, in the relative minor, 2/4. This contrasts sharply with the caressing tenderness of the preceding, by unexpected changes of key, accent, and general character. A strongly accented figure in the bass involves the lengthening of the third and fourth bars of the theme in an animated argument. An arrogant bellicose cadence a little later paves the way for a dramatic entry of the second section in the right hand.

Variation III, 6/16. A return to the tonality of D major and to the melodic character of the first variation, similar use of four-part writing.

But here an idealized version of the theme is stated in the lower part, unfolding in the sensitive middle register of the piano, while the three upper voices link together to form a finely-woven and flexible accompaniment. Then by analogy with the formation of the theme, the second section is made up by the entire inversion of this arrangement. The cantabile phrase of the bass moves, inverted, to the upper part in the right hand; the other parts now become a sinuous accompaniment, fit in with this shifting redistribution, and move downwards.

Variation IV, D major, 4/4. The melody here stretches out in its entire length beneath a light figure of triplet quavers which seem in their pattern to continue the outline of the preceding variation. It appears first in the right hand, spurred on by rich syncopations which oddly disintegrate the original rhythm. A statement in the left hand follows in its turn, enclosed in rare harmonies, up to a point in the variation where it merges into the second section of the theme, when the right hand takes it again to the end.

Variation V, *lent*, in D major, 3/4. Only the spirit of the theme, disembodied, hovers over this obscure variation; its original basis survives merely in the presence of a three-note phrase, of expressive character, which is seen to be a melodic extension of the trill that unites the second and third bars of the first section. This phrase forms the germ of a contemplative development of serious and unusual beauty.

Variation VI, in D major, 3/4. Here, again, there seems to be a wide gulf between the theme and its emanations. There remains of the original melody only one or two fragmentary designs in thirds derived from its fourth bar, which crop up here and there as a provocative ornament to the play of an entirely new melody incorporated in this variation with freshness and charm.

Here concludes the first subdivision of the variations. These tend as a whole to amplify the melodic possibilities of the theme, as I have already indicated and as this rapid analysis shows. In the group which follows, the composer's intention is clearly to develop the theme on its rhythmic side.

Variation VII, in D major, 4/4, *assez vif*. Although the theme is at no time stated in the course of this variation, which bubbles over with a charming bravura and vivacity, it is present throughout as the conscious force controlling the sound-pattern behind which it unfolds.

If, against each bar of the variation, the reader mentally sets the corresponding bar of the theme, he will become aware of the clear outline of the unheard minuet beneath the lively play of ornament and the deceptive rhythm which is no longer its own, and sense its form through the impenetrable veil that wraps it round.

Variation VIII, 4/4. Still in D major, but in a state of perpetual modulation. The allusions to the theme are very free. A rhythmic figure in the right hand, on a moving base of demisemiquavers, states the first bar of the subject in augmentation, then finishes by recalling the fourth bar. At the same time the left hand outlines in an appoggiatura form the very much truncated melodic scheme of the first section. These fragmentary figures reappear in the course of the variation, but they are not developed.

Variation IX, in D major, 9/8. A lively *divertisse-ment* in merry rhythm for the right hand, matching the candid statement of the theme in the left. Here the theme constantly reappears, easily recognizable in spite of the modification imposed by the vivacity of triple time.

Variation X, in D major, 3/4. At first sight one might think this variation entirely detached from the theme, so self-contained and personal is its character. All that remains seems to be the strong harmonic foundation, on which a weighty motif unfolds its luxuriant design. Yet from the phrase for the left hand, though it keeps up this apparent detachment, can be disentangled the first three bars of the original theme in ornamental amplification. The linked variations forming the second group conclude on this expansively rhythmic note.

Variation XI, in D minor, 3/4. *Sombre, assez lent.* This variation forms a preparation to the Interlude and consequently to the Finale itself, and opens in an atmosphere of heavy, inscrutable shadow. The wailing little figure that forms its base is a chromatic distortion of the third bar of the theme and struggles in a dragging backwash of harmonies. For a moment its persistent plaint drowns the accompaniment, but

Paul Dukas

it fades and dies away in the uneasy lull of a tonic pedal. A second motif rises to the surface, petrified by a succession of icy common chords, a half-spectral phrase recalling the melodic scheme already noticed in the eighth variation.

A modulation to G minor follows, then a curious pause in which there echoes like a far-off call the characteristic interval of a falling third which is to usher in the Finale. In conclusion, there is a recapitulation of the initial episode, linking on this time to the Interlude.

This section of the work introduces into it a note of dramatic emotion surprising in the style that prevails. By a further audacity, we are to find, in the Interlude, the Variation in the form of improvisation. It is highly, stylized, and draws largely on the principal theme. As in the introduction to the Finale of the Sonata, the composer's caprice brings various motifs into play, testing them one after the other in a summary development, and keeping one only, which is moulded to a point of perfection where it serves as the foundation of a main exposition. In this search through imaginative resources, the theme of Rameau—or rather the thematic fragments drawn from it—is naturally the object of skilful modifications which distinguish it from the previous variations. This is an added problem before the composer—the variation of the variation—and one which he achieves so triumphantly that the only impression we gain from this extraordinary section of his work is its moving beauty.

Leaving the key of D minor already established in the eleventh variation, a succession of modulations becoming continually more lucid and more decided, based rhythmically on the first bar and melodically on the three following bars, carry the two main elements of the theme to the bright clarity of D major, in which is asserted the triumphant motif ushering in the Finale. This passage from shadow into light is achieved with rare harmony of inspiration and reasoned logic. It is a moment of a unique quality which alone is enough to place the work on its proper level.

The working out of feeling in the course of this episode has determined unalterably the character of the pages to come, forming the twelfth variation or Finale, which is its natural extension and directly linked to it. From now onwards a sentiment of joy and regained pace prevails till the end of the work.

The theme reappears in its entirety, covered with glory and, as Vincent d'Indy remarks, 'amplified to giant proportions'. But it is preceded by the broad, detailed exposition of the lively motif which is later to act as its contrapuntal support, prancing gaily through the whole of this last development. This motif is marked by an odd lack of balance; a sort of syncopated leap involves a continual alternation of accents on strong and weak beats in the upper part; but it is a complete synthesis of the first section of the subject, stressing particularly the rhythmic element of the fourth bar. The ingenious play of imitation keeps up the interest of the preliminary *divertissement* until the point where the original

Paul Dukas

minuet subject, reappearing phrase by phrase, first in
E flat, and then in F major, brings back the glamour
of ceremonious dance rhythm.

Then the two subjects are set in juxtaposition, the
theme of the Variation and the original theme—the
latter this time given completely in its original key—
uniting for a final sonorous peroration, unrolling
tonal imagery and almost orchestral colour, which
crowns this perfect work; it concludes with a satirical
thrust at the first flourish of the minuet.

In no other genre than that of the Variation could
Paul Dukas better have demonstrated his extraordinary
gift for controlling and marshalling his resources.
All the qualities that stamp his peculiarly individual
talent, constructive power, deductive reasoning,
and abundant capacity for thematic development,
unite here to the greater glory of a technique that
of itself is already a thing of beauty. I have tried
to define some of its elements, but my analysis is
inadequate if it has not also conveyed the throb
of a sensitive inspiration beneath the surface perfection of method.

The success of this work was marked by two successive editions. Misled by the label of 'New
Edition' which the second, dated 1907, bears, one
might expect to find in it some modification of detail due to the indefatigable zeal of a composer well
versed in the precept of Boileau. Schumann and
Liszt have accustomed us to these retouched ver-
sions, following the original publication. But here
there is nothing of the sort. Even the original
printer's errors of the first edition are faithfully

reproduced, and one cannot see exactly where its alleged newness lies.

There remains to discuss the two short pieces which I have kept aside to study on account of their difference in style and dimensions from those I have just analysed. Both were composed in similar circumstances.

In 1910, anniversary of the death of Haydn, the Revue S.I.M., edited by Jules Écorcheville, published a musical supplement under the title of 'Hommage à Haydn', in which several musicians of note participated: Vincent d'Indy, Debussy, Ravel, Dukas, Reynaldo Hahn, Ch. M. Widor. All the compositions in this collection bore the same characteristic of being constructed on a musical rendering of the letters of Haydn's name. That is to say, in the Anglo-German notation, H interpreted as si, A as la, D as ré, and Y and N corresponding, by a somewhat arbitrary application of the alphabet to the diatonic scale, to ré and sol.

Dukas's contribution is represented by a *Prélude élégiaque* of only a few lines. It would be difficult to find more than ingenuity here, outside the technical grace with which he treats the problem before them all. It would be out of place to expect more.

In 1920, immediately after the *Revue Musicale* was founded, Henry Prunières's first gesture was to dedicate a special number of his journal to the memory of Claude Debussy. This number, the second published, appeared in December 1920, and is now almost impossible to obtain. Attached to it was a

Paul Dukas

booklet bearing the title *Tombeau de Claude Debussy*, in which Prunières, reviving an old custom of the lutenists so dear to him, had collected together a series of musical pieces by composers chosen by reason of their spiritual affinity to the composer of *Pelléas*. France was represented here by Dukas, Roussel, Florent Schmitt, Ravel, and Erik Satie, the foreign world by Malipiero, Goossens, Béla Bartòk, Stravinsky, and de Falla. The choice was a fine one, and the artistic outcome worthy of the motive behind it. Here, it is true, it was not a question of a *divertissement* on four notes. The theme proposed was a more moving one, the thought of the near and poignant sorrow that the art of music, with full heart and tenderest feeling, had just sustained.

Dukas's piece, which opens the set, is called *La plainte, au loin, du Faune . . .*' as though Dukas had endeavoured to come as close as possible to the style of his dead friend even in his choice of title. It is impossible to imagine the more moving evocation of a style or the more intimate understanding of a lyrical spirit than is revealed here in these few pages steeped in sad tenderness. The personalities of Debussy and of Dukas are here merged together to a degree that the sensuous pastoral plaint of the *Prélude à l'Après-midi*, with its drowsy chromaticism from which the whole piece grows, is suddenly recreated here in a mood of oriental languor—an echo of *La Péri*, we notice on re-reading that work. The sheer quality of this work is far above the usual merit of pieces written to occasion. It is often included on the programmes of countless pianists who find in its interpretation the twofold pleasure of paying homage to the memory of a great musician while marvelling at the art of the composer who is singing his praise.

Jacques Durand has published these two short works in an edition more readable than was possible in the journal, owing to its small dimensions. Let us look forward to reading before long in his catalogue under the name of Paul Dukas the title of a new piano work as significant of his ripe talent as the Sonata and the Variations have been of his aspirations hitherto. These fine compositions have been magnificent milestones on the road of French music. There still remains for their composer a long and glorious road to travel. May he never forget to mark it out by fresh witnesses of his interest in the instrument whose resources he has so nobly employed, whose expressive capacity he has so broadly understood.